Praise for *Hope, Not Fear: A Path to Jewish Renaissance*

"Serves as an uplifting introduction to the people, institutions, issues, and ideas that promise to reshape the North American Jewish community of the twenty-first century."
—Jonathan D. Sarna, Ph.D., Joseph H. & Belle R. Braun Professor of American Jewish History, Brandeis University, and author of *American Judaism*

"A wise book by a Jewish leader who loves Jews and Judaism alike.... This thoughtful, insightful meditation ... fills one with a sense of hope about the Jewish future."
—Rabbi Joseph Telushkin, author of *A Code of Jewish Ethics* and *Jewish Literacy*

"Reading this groundbreaking book will reward you with actual answers to the most pressing questions for the North American Jewish community."   —Dara Horn, author of *All Other Nights*

"Bronfman's hoping his latest crusade will prove to be his most important legacy. So keep your eye on him."
—Ami Eden, *Jewish Telegraphic Agency*

"Arguing that a place should be available for everyone who wants to be under the tent is not a new idea, but Bronfman presents this point with vigor and candor.... Bronfman advises respect for all the individual ways in which people choose to be Jewish and practice their faith."
—Stephen Mark Dobbs, *J Weekly*

HOPE,
NOT FEAR

A Path to Jewish Renaissance

EDGAR M. BRONFMAN
and BETH ZASLOFF

St. Martin's Griffin
New York

www.stmartins.com

Book design by Gretchen Achilles

The Library of Congress has cataloged the hardcover edition as follows:

Bronfman, Edgar M., Zasloff, Beth.
  Hope, not fear : a path to Jewish renaissance / Edgar M. Bronfman and Beth Zasloff.—1st ed.
    p. cm.
  ISBN 978-0-312-37792-2
  1. Judaism—North America. 2. Judaism—21st century. 3. Jewish way of life. 4. Jews—North America—Identity. 5. Jews—North America—Social conditions—21st century. 6. Jewish youth—Religious life—North America. 7. Jewish leadership—North America. 8. North America—Ethnic relations. I. Title.

                                              2008020996

ISBN 978-0-312-59889-1 (trade paperback)

First St. Martin's Griffin Edition: November 2010

To my brother, Charles, and his departed wife, Andrea;
and to my sons Matthew and Adam—
all toilers in the same Jewish vineyard

CONTENTS

CONTENTS

HOW THIS BOOK WAS WRITTEN

This book comes out of several years of thinking, writing, and conversations about the current shape and future of contemporary Jewish life. My own ideas and observations were clarified, deepened, and frequently changed by what I learned over the course of more than seventy interviews with individuals who are passionately concerned about our Jewish future. They taught me much from their own experience and dedication. I am enormously grateful to these people—communal leaders, professors, rabbis, educators, and students—many of whom came to my office in New York or to the King David Hotel in Jerusalem, and who permitted me to tape our interviews so that I could further reflect on their insights.

I have been very fortunate in the writing of this book to have had the collaboration of Beth Zasloff, a gifted writer and teacher of writing, and an alumna from one of the first years of the Bronfman Youth Fellowships, a program that

I began in 1987. She helped to seek out experts on issues important to the book and participated in the interviews. Over e-mail, I sent her what I wrote on themes I distilled from these conversations. Beth and I exchanged ideas, and she shaped my writing into the chapters that follow. The result is a real intergenerational partnership.

PREFACE TO THE NEW EDITION

Hope, Not Fear: A Path to Jewish Renaissance

Soon after the first edition of *Hope, Not Fear* was published, in September 2008, many asked me if my sense of hope had diminished. That winter brought a new season of anxiety in the Jewish community, as the plummeting economy and the revelation of Bernard Madoff's Ponzi scheme dealt an enormous blow to the finances of many Jewish organizations. But a financial crisis should not mean a crisis of vision. The future of North American Jewry depends on our ability to make Jewish life relevant for successive generations. The signs that the American Jewish community has indeed begun on a path to Jewish renaissance can be read not in the financial health of Jewish organizations, but in the energy and commitment of Jewish youth. Over the past two years, new, creative efforts by visionary Jewish leaders have shown that given the opportunity, young American Jews are ready to bring Judaism into their lives, and bring new life to American Judaism.

This winter, I was struck by the innovation I saw in celebrations of the holiday Tu b'Shvat, which in recent decades
has been reenvisioned as the Jewish "Earth Day." The date,
cited by the rabbis of the Talmud to mark the "new year of
the trees," was first established as a festival by the Kabbalists,
or Jewish mystics, who celebrated spiritual connection to the
land and fruits of Israel. With the rise of Zionism in the late
nineteenth century, Jews around the world began to mark
the day by planting a tree in Palestine. In increasing numbers,
American Jews now participate in contemporary versions of
the Kabbalistic Tu b'Shvat seder, but with a focus that has
moved from the land of Israel to the earth as a whole. Guests
at the seder drink four cups of wine, feast on fruits and nuts,
and explore, in song and prayer, what Judaism teaches about
the role of human beings in the natural world, from theological concepts about the interconnectedness of creation to
biblical and Talmudic prohibitions against waste. As more
recognize the damage human beings have inflicted on our
planet, this "new year" brings resolutions to take part in *tikkun
olam,* the repair of the world.

The transformations of Tu b'Shvat are an example that
reflects both the changing character of the Jewish people and
the adaptability of the Jewish tradition. For Jews in North
America, the past decades have brought an unprecedented
condition of success and welcome. But with little societal
anti-Semitism to remind them that they are Jewish, young
Jews increasingly regard their Judaism as less central to their
identities than did Jews of earlier generations. High levels of

assimilation and intermarriage have caused many to fear that Judaism in America will fade into insignificance. I wrote *Hope, Not Fear* to express my conviction that this need not be the case. Young Jews may see their Judaism as only one strand among their diverse attachments, and express greater commitment to social and environmental causes than to working on behalf of the Jewish people. But they possess a strong interest in how their heritage is relevant to their lives and, given the opportunity, can create a new kind of American Judaism. The reinvented Tu b'Shvat seder speaks to young people in the way it explores universally relevant ideas through the deeply rooted language of Jewish tradition. That young Jews find pride and joy in this tradition gives me hope for a vibrant Jewish future.

The Jewish community can and should do more with less. While the coffers of some long-established organizations have been emptied, young Jews have created highly popular new efforts on shoestring budgets. In a 2008 survey called *The Innovation Ecosystem,* the organization Jumpstart identified more than 300 geographically diverse Jewish start-ups, including small nonprofits and independent *minyans,* or prayer groups, that in 2008 alone reached more than 400,000 people. These efforts vary in their missions, but share a welcoming, inclusive ethos, a spiritual dynamism, and a focus on environmental and social issues.

Established organizations have begun to recognize that if they are to reach young people, a new openness must replace the old tribalism. This means welcoming Jews of many backgrounds, and exploring how Judaism can help approach significant issues in people's lives and in the world. For example, Hillel: the Foundation for Jewish Campus Life has expanded its work in social service, most recently through an "Urban Alternative Break" created in partnership with City Year, a secular national service organization. Using the successful model of Hillel's existing "alternative break" program, students combine twenty-five hours of service in at-risk urban communities with an educational program and a peer-led Shabbat experience. Another new initiative brings "senior educators" to campuses to reach out to students on the periphery of Jewish life. The educators help students connect to Jewish experiences like Birthright Israel and lead learning sessions that explore Jewish responses to philosophical and ethical questions.

Jewish renaissance is above all about Jewish learning, and new technologies have brought innovative ways to connect people to Jewish study and to each other. The Web site MyJewishLearning.com, which offers a wide array of information and perspectives on Judaism, has seen its visitors exponentially increase in the past year. The Web site does not dictate what it means to be a "good Jew," but offers all who are interested the opportunity to pursue Jewish learning. The Talmudic maxim, "Make for yourself a teacher," should guide any approach to Jewish education. If Jews of a new generation are given opportunities to take ownership of their Judaism, they will find ways to transform received wisdom into vibrant new forms.

My teacher this past Tu b'Shvat was Rabbi Arthur Green, who led one of the weekly text study sessions that I discuss in the pages that follow. Together with students and faculty from the transdenominational Hebrew College Rabbinical School, which Rabbi Green founded, we read ancient and modern texts that explore the cycle of the seasons. They included this beautiful quote about springtime from the biblical Song of Songs:

> My beloved spoke thus to me: "Arise, my darling; my fair one, come away! For winter is past, the rains are over and gone. The blossoms have appeared in the land, the time of pruning has come; the song of the turtledove is heard in our land.

The rabbis of the Talmud read the lines as an allegory for the Jewish people's redemption from slavery in Egypt. "The winter is past" is interpreted as, "This winter is the four hundred years of slavery decreed upon our ancestors." This interpretation first struck me as at odds with the poetry of the lines. In the world of Judaism, narratives of suffering can seem to cast a shadow over even the most joyful imagery.

But the text and its interpretation also speak to a Jewish understanding of renewal and rebirth, a central element in Jewish tradition and practice. Jewish foundational narratives tell story after story of moving from bondage to freedom, from wrongdoing to redemption. Every week, Shabbat, the day of rest, offers a time to breathe, reflect, rejoice, and then begin again. Jewish life cycle ceremonies and festivals mark the growth of the individual and the yearly cycle of the seasons. Like the Tu b'Shvat seder, they celebrate connectedness and regeneration. A vibrant Jewish practice can be a transformative force for the individual and the world. The American Jewish community must recognize the seeds of new life that have begun to flourish, and cultivate a Jewish renaissance. This book is my gesture of hope, for the renewal of the Jewish people and of the world we share.

—Edgar M. Bronfman
August, 2010

HOPE, NOT FEAR

INTRODUCTION

Every Thursday afternoon, a diverse group of ten or twelve people meets at my office to study Jewish texts. Regular participants include rabbis, Jewish communal leaders, students, and young professionals. Some may be Orthodox; others might have had little contact with Jewish life since their teenage years. Guided by a rabbi or professor, we delve into the texts of our tradition, reading them line by line and debating their meaning. The subjects of our study might seem arcane: a Talmudic story about Rav Eleazar Ben Doria, who chased after prostitutes; a ruling about the legal status of the *mamzer,* or bastard; an analysis of a Biblical text concerning the treatment of the Gibeonites, a tribe condemned by Joshua to carry water for the Jewish priests; Biblical readings on how the Israelites celebrated victories and harvests. As we explore the nuances of the texts, we invariably find ourselves addressing key topics that face our Jewish community today. How do we treat the outsider? How do we balance the needs of our own people with a larger commitment to human rights? How do we negotiate respect for tradition while adapting to a changing world? How should we mourn and how should we celebrate? Even as I struggle with difficult texts, I always get a pang of pride when I think that for so many centuries our people have been grappling with these central questions, always seeking both justice and joy.

My regular Jewish study has been more than a source of great meaning and fulfillment in my own life. It has been deeply intertwined with what I consider the most important task in North American Jewish life today: to foster a renaissance of Jewish learning and culture. The pride I feel in my religion is all too rare among North American Jews, who are opting out of their Jewishness at alarming rates. Pride requires knowledge, and most Jews, while sophisticated in many subjects, are ignorant about Judaism. In the past, anti-Semitism ensured that Jews knew they were Jews, whether they liked it or not. Now that we have been so thoroughly integrated into North American life, young Jews can choose whether to identify themselves as Jewish, but they must know enough about their tradition to do so. If we are to guarantee a significant Jewish future, we now need substantive, broad-based Jewish education, so that Judaism, which has stayed alive through so much adversity, may grow and thrive in an open society.

While I have fought Jewish persecution throughout my life, I now see that the fight against anti-Semitism, which occupied Jewish organized life for a century, is no longer the most urgent matter. What North American Jews need now is hope, not fear. We have to build, not fight. We need to celebrate the joy in Judaism, even as we recognize our responsibility to alleviate suffering and to help heal a broken world. We need to understand Judaism as a multifaceted culture as well as a religion, and explore Jewish literature, music, and art. We need to understand our tradition of debate and questioning, and invite all to enter a conversation about our central texts, rituals, and laws. We need to open our book anew, and re-create a vital Judaism for our time.

In my father's generation of Jews in North America, Jews clung together out of a sense of necessity as well as a sense of peoplehood, turning to their Jewish family to provide support in a society where anti-Semitism was a fact of life, and to offer international aid during an era that would see the murder of 6 million Jews. For my father, to be Jewish meant to fear attack. Today, with the freedom and acceptance that Jews enjoy in this country, we have the chance to bring our family together not for mutual protection, but for a shared celebration of our common heritage.

Let's set aside the conviction that the world will always hate us, and instead delve into our texts, ethics, culture, and religion to understand how we can help fight hatred in the world. Let's use our knowledge of persecution—and our techniques for fighting it—in service of others who are suffering, Jews and non-Jews. In doing so, we would be true to our tradition, which makes us responsible to our own family, but also to all of our fellow human beings. If we make Judaism an active part of our lives today and pass it on to the next generation, it would be a great service not only to the Jewish people, but to all humanity.

Fostering Jewish renaissance is a different kind of work than securing freedom for Jews who are oppressed, or seeking justice for victims of anti-Semitism. Yet in taking on this task, we must adopt the same sense of urgency that has made North American Jews such effective advocates for Jews in danger worldwide. Nobody is going to die of assimilation, but we are in danger of losing the religion and culture that have helped so many to lead better lives, and to better the lives of so many others. It's not too late to act, but we must act now.

What can we do to push against the tide and bring new life to Judaism? The answer has to be a new kind of Jewish education. For many Jews today, Jewish education has meant Hebrew school lessons about a history of suffering and a series of incomprehensible rituals. We must teach our children about our painful history and ensure that neither they nor all the world's children forget the Holocaust. But the Jewish education of the new millennium must also teach that ours is a joyous religion, one that celebrates the life of the individual as well as the seasons of the year. It should open the door to our rich texts, rituals, and traditions, and welcome all who wish to participate in reading, understanding, and questioning them. It should celebrate Judaism's positive contributions to society, and its imperative that we leave the world a better place than we found it.

For most of my life, this notion of Jewish education would have seemed completely foreign. As I was growing up, my knowledge of Judaism was limited to lessons for my bar mitzvah and attendance at a junior congregation that I found dull and pointless, especially since I knew that my father did not attend synagogue on Saturdays—he went to the office instead. The final straw for me was when I realized that while my father and his brothers could read Hebrew with the speed of summer lightning, they didn't understand a word of it. As an adult, I spurned religious practice and raised my own children in a home where Judaism was almost completely absent. At the same time, in my public life I immersed myself in Jewish causes, responding to the cataclysmic changes of the twentieth century, which saw the Holocaust, the founding of the State of Israel, and the fall of Communism. I felt a responsibility to fight for Jews worldwide but little connection to the content of Jewish religion and culture. Slowly, my involvement in Jewish life led me to appreciate that something more than the fight against anti-Semitism had kept our religion alive while so many others faded away. I witnessed thousands of Jews gathered outside Moscow's Choral Synagogue for the holiday Simchat Torah, and marveled over the fact that despite years of suppressing religion in the Soviet Union these Jews still celebrated this joyful holiday. Starting in my sixties, I began to make changes in my life. I lit Shabbat candles with my wife every Friday night. I stopped eating pork and shellfish to assert my Jewish identity. I became a proud Jew, in my home and in my heart.

I also began to learn. With the help of rabbis, teachers, and other students of many ages, I embarked on a quest for

knowledge that does not cease to enthrall me. I look forward
every week to the Thursday study sessions. Members of the
group are mostly a lot younger than me, which pleases me no
end, and come from a range of Jewish backgrounds. The joy
of learning comes equally from the encounter with the
voices of our ancient tradition and the dynamic exchange
among a diverse group of my fellow Jews.

One session, for example, was led by Rabbi Sharon Cohen Anisfeld, together with rabbinical students from Hebrew College in Boston, where she is dean. The texts we read
were from the portion of the Mishnah, or Oral Law, called
Pirkei Avot, "Ethics of Our Fathers." Judaism has long been
concerned, Cohen Anisfeld opened by saying, with the problem that even when we know what is right, we don't do it. In
compiling the ethical wisdom of several generations of leading rabbis, Pirkei Avot asks us: "How do we create a frame of
consciousness that leads to moral behavior?"

The texts we read all deal in some way with how we define
ourselves in relation to others, like the following teaching of
Rabbi Hillel: "Do not separate yourself from the community;
do not rely on yourself until the day of your death; do not
judge your fellow until you reach his situation."[1]

The text is striking in the way it seems to insist that we
submit our own will to that of others. It seems to go against
values many of us hold dear: our independence, our ability to
judge, and the particularly American value of self-reliance.
We discussed these tensions. Are not the greatest thinkers
precisely those who separate from the community? one stu-

dent asked. Is Hillel asking us to withhold judgment of others, since, after all, you can never stand in another's exact situation? If so, how do we effect justice when we know a wrong has been committed? Does the last line open the door to a kind of moral relativism that explains away all wrongdoing?

None of these questions have easy answers. Yet I can't believe that Hillel is asking us to completely submerge our own wills and judgments. After all, he also taught the famous and beautiful words, "If I am not for myself, who will be for me? And if I am only for myself, then what am I? And, if not now, when?"[2] Instead, the lines voice a fundamental sense that to be human is to exist in relation to other human beings. This relationship can and must be governed by understanding and empathy. The attempt to imagine the experience of another is the first step to ethical action, and it is fundamental to Judaism, as expressed in the words from Exodus: "You shall not oppress a stranger; for you know the feelings of the stranger, having yourselves been strangers in the land of Egypt."[3] To insist on our connection to, reliance on, and empathy for our fellow human beings is to insist on a society where we can never close our hearts to others, where justice is never an abstract concept but bound up in our shared experience of being human.

There is a thrill to finding the contemporary relevance in our ancient texts, and to hearing the ancient echoes in our contemporary debates. We did not leave the room agreeing on the meaning of Hillel's words, and we each returned home to a different kind of Jewish practice, ranging from secular to Orthodox. But in joining together to read and discuss Pirkei Avot, we were creating a Jewish community of learning, thinking, and ethical concern. One need not be an expert in Judaism to delve into its texts and traditions, at any age. Jewish renaissance means opening up new ways for Jews to connect to their ancient tradition and to each other, so that we foster a flowering of a newly energetic Jewish life.

Many wonderful organizations and teachers are providing meaningful encounters with Judaism and with the Jewish people, through summer camps, college programs, day schools, youth organizations, and synagogue programs, among other venues. But we still have a long way to go if we are to ensure that all Jews have the opportunity to experience a joyful and meaningful Jewish life. I am very much involved in programs and projects that aim to do this, and I will discuss some of these initiatives in this book, as I set forth my views of what must be done to build a significant Jewish future in North America.

In the process of writing this book, I have interviewed men and women who are working to foster Jewish renaissance. They have taught me a great deal, both about the ideas at the heart of a renaissance in Jewish life and about the important and exciting work that is under way. Many of these conversations are recounted as I set forth my own conclusions and recommendations.

Part I of the book describes the spirit that should guide a Jewish renaissance. It offers the North American Jewish community a hopeful vision for an inclusive, welcoming Judaism. Part 2 addresses the question of how we make a renaissance happen, and discusses the place where, above all, Jewish renaissance must take place: in the Jewish home.

The book's title came out of one of my first meetings with Richard Joel, the charismatic former leader of Hillel: The Foundation for Jewish Campus Life. As Joel and I prepared to work together in what would become a tremendously fruitful partnership at Hillel, I told him that there was one thing I wanted him to remember. This was the phrase "hope, not fear." It was a spontaneous thought, which I had not previously put into words. It expressed the conviction that fear, the operating system of Jews for centuries, is no longer a motivating force for North American Jews. No young person is going to become more Jewish because of fear of Jewish disappearance. Without "the others" to remind us, through persecution and exclusion, that we are Jews, we need to find positive, hopeful ways to affirm and perpetuate our own Judaism.

There is a second sense in which "hope, not fear" is used in the book. This is with regard to the high rates of intermarriage in North America. Some who are concerned for our Jewish future see intermarriage as the new enemy and call for increased efforts to stop it. We have to accept the reality: In an open society, people will fall in love. The ghettoization of Jews that made intermarriage unthinkable for earlier generations no longer exists today, and we do not want to re-create it. Instead of fearing intermarriage, we should be confident in the strength of our tradition and welcome the partners of our youth who are not Jewish. If we welcome them with love, instead of that suspicious, supercilious manner I have so often seen, they will be more likely to raise their children as Jews and may even decide to convert to Judaism themselves. Our fight should be directed toward ignorance, not at intermarriage, with the hope that more knowledge will bring a stronger commitment to passing on Judaism to the next generation.

To awaken in the morning and not know what you are going to do that day is a punishment I hope I never deserve. Since I retired from the Seagram Company Ltd. in 1994, I have been absorbed in my work for the Jewish people, primarily as president of the World Jewish Congress and as chairman of Hillel's International Board of Governors. In June 2007, I resigned my position at the World Jewish Congress. As my seventy-eighth birthday was almost upon me, it was more than time to pass the baton, and I am content that the legacy is in good hands. In the time left to me, I will continue my work with Hillel and other efforts that aim to make the richness of Judaism available to all. There are other things I could be doing, but Jewish renaissance is where I feel I have special talents, a special background, and a deep yearning to bring Jews back from the brink of peaceful extinction.

Jews have contributed so much to the world, and we have much more to contribute. Not only is Judaism the source of monotheism, the Ten Commandments, and the Torah, or Law, but Jews have also contributed out of all proportion to their numbers in science, the arts, and the humanities. There are more Jewish Nobel Laureates than any other single ethnic group, despite the fact that there are only some 14 million of us. Jews have often led the way in making the world a better place: We see ourselves as partners with God in creation, with a God-given commandment that we call *tzedek*, meaning "justice." Our Talmud dictates how all of us can live in justice with our fellow human beings. It was written some thousand years before the English common law that gave rise to democracy. If we are indeed the chosen people, we are chosen to be a light unto the nations and to lead them down the paths of justice. Unfortunately, we are still in training and have yet to put our own house in order before attempting to lead others.

At this juncture in our history, North American Jewry is in dire need of a new vision for itself, one that can steer the different elements of this complicated small but noisy people. This book is an attempt to set forth that vision. I am not a prophet, nor a learned rabbi, nor a Nobel Laureate. I am a proud Jew who senses a need and am trying my best to follow my star in the time left to me. In my seventy-eight years, I have accumulated much experience and many friends and I have studied with many learned men and women. I now have the chutzpah to try to tell others what they must do. I apologize for that, but I am doing it anyway.

That is who I am. I will spend the rest of my days working to push the renaissance, hoping to get more and more young Jews invested in their tradition, in their culture. The words "hope, not fear" still resonate within me. We must look to the

future with hope. Talmud teaches us that even if we can't fin-
ish the task in our lifetime, neither can we shirk from giving
it our all. After me there will come others who will feel the
same zeal, the same feeling of inner peace, as they toil in
these same vineyards.

Part I

———⇒◦◦◦⇐———

THE SPIRIT
OF A
JEWISH
RENAISSANCE

Chapter 1

A GOLDEN AGE FOR
NORTH AMERICAN JEWRY?

When the great mass of Jews immigrated to the United States and Canada in the late nineteenth and early twentieth centuries, they didn't come in order to be better Jews. They came in search of a better life, eager to leave behind the poverty and anti-Semitism in those areas of Eastern Europe where Jews were permitted to settle. It was most important to speak English, support their families, and give their children a good education. The rallying cry was not "Be Jewish," but "Be somebody!"

Jewish identity, for these immigrants, was not something that had to be learned or strengthened. It was a condition of life, defined by their experience of anti-Semitism and separation from the larger society. They didn't worry about whether their children would remain Jewish. They assumed that like them, the next generation would simply have no choice in the matter; North American society would not accept them other than as Jews. So while they taught their children to fight for the rights of the Jewish people—and of all humanity—to live in freedom, they taught them little of the texts, history, and traditions of Judaism.

If we examine the matter more closely, we will find that the great majority of the immigrants were themselves mostly ignorant about Judaism. As the late Arthur Hertzberg describes in *The Jews in America*, the Eastern European Jews who came to North America were "penniless and largely uneducated even in Judaism."[1] The shtetls from which they had come were organized so that the very few who knew Hebrew and could study Torah did so in the *beit midrash*, the study hall. Those students of Torah and Talmud were highly respected, and studying was what they did all day, while their wives struggled to feed the family. The others were taught to read Hebrew but not to understand it. They spoke Yiddish and went to synagogue and prayed, having no idea what they were saying when they chanted the service. Is it any wonder that learning Judaism took a backseat when they came to the United States and Canada?

While their new home offered the first generation of Jewish immigrants far greater freedom and opportunity than the "old country," they still faced discrimination and hate. In response, the Jewish communal agenda focused on fighting anti-Semitism and ensuring a secure, prosperous future for the Jews. Institutions such as the Anti-Defamation League of B'nai Brith struggled to make the anti-Semitism in North American society, as depicted in the film *Gentleman's Agreement*, fade away. Organizations were built to support the needs of new immigrants, to advocate for Jews in North America and worldwide, and, later, to support the young State of Israel.

To what would have been the great surprise of our immigrant grandparents, we Jews have succeeded beyond their dearest hopes. Jews have reached positions of leadership and status in many fields. In government, an Orthodox Jew, Joseph Lieberman, has been a serious vice presidential candidate and contender for the presidential nomination. In business, Jews are in senior positions in manufacturing companies, in banks and investment banking firms, and in service companies. In education, countless Jews are professors at North America's universities, and a number of Ivy League colleges have Jewish presidents. When I went to Williams College, class of 1950, I said to myself that long before there would be a Jewish president of that noble educational institution there would be a Jewish president of the United States. Now Morton Owen Schapiro, the second Jewish president of Williams, welcomes students into his home to celebrate the Passover seder. Not only have Jews achieved economic and professional success in North American society, but being Jewish has also lost its stigma. Ethnic identity, once seen as something to be shed in the melting pot of North American life, is now celebrated. Love has replaced hate, as non-Jews use the Jewish Internet dating site, JDate, to find Jewish spouses. Jewish holidays are respected in schools and in the workplace. While anti-Semitism certainly has not disappeared entirely, it is no longer a significant force in North American life.

In the view of many, the North American Jewish community has reached a golden age that far eclipses any golden age in the long history of Jewry. But for those of us who care about the future of Judaism, the news isn't so good. Something was lost in the transition from the shtetl to the condominium. North America's warm welcome has led to a new kind of danger: the danger that without others forcing our identity upon us, we will forget who we are. In the past, "the others" made sure that Jews knew they were Jewish. Now that we are free to choose Judaism, our existence is threatened not by the others but by the ease with which we ourselves seem to cast off Jewish identity. "Who is a Jew?" has been the hotly debated question in past decades: Is a Jew a person with a Jewish mother? A Jewish father? A Jewish grandparent? Now the question "Who is a Jew?" is slowly being answered by "a person whose grandchildren are Jewish."

My mentor Nahum Goldmann had a wise expression: When things are good for Jews, it's bad for Jewry. Yes, it is a golden age for Jews in North America, with greater prosperity and recognition and fewer physical dangers than ever before. But we now must ask, do North America's rapidly assimilating Jews possess a Jewish identity that is durable enough for their children's children to inherit?

Richard Joel, former president and international director of Hillel, now president of Yeshiva University, would say that being Jewish used to be a condition and now it's an option. How very true. When I was young, I was Jewish because my parents were Jewish, as were theirs. For me, Judaism is what Rabbi David Ellenson, president of the Hebrew Union College–Jewish Institute of Religion (HUC–JIR), called a "habit of the heart," a deep, inseparable part of where I come from and who I am. "We grew up as either children or grand-children of immigrants," Ellenson told me. In that context, he said, "'Do I choose to be Jewish?' was an absurd kind of question."

When I asked Rabbi David Hartman, founder and co-director of the Shalom Hartman Institute in Jerusalem, to put into words the biggest problem the Jewish people face, his answer was, "How to survive with freedom . . . When Jews were being persecuted, they had a way of coping with suffering. Now the issue is not suffering. The issue is the freedom to become anything you want while living in an open society which doesn't constrain you."

Is there something that we can do to keep Judaism alive, and significant, in North America? Yes, if we care enough. But first we must recognize just how serious the situation is. For Judaism to survive with the freedom Jews now enjoy, we must unite to fight the new enemies: our own ignorance and apathy. If we can cure the apathy about Judaism, then we will be able to cure the ignorance. It's not too late to act, but the prognosis is not good if we do not.

I dreamed up the phrase "Jewish renaissance" with Richard Joel when I first began my work with Hillel in 1994. We used it to describe what we wanted to accomplish at Hillel and throughout the Jewish educational system. (We thought of "rejuvenation" and discarded it as a pun in bad taste.) At the time, the Jewish community was still reeling from the 1990 National Jewish Population Survey, which reported an intermarriage rate of over 50 percent. The immediate response was panic, as the Jewish community asked itself, "How do we keep our children Jewish?" "Jewish continuity" became the new communal buzzword.

As a slogan, "Jewish continuity" lacks vigor and challenge. What are we asking young Jews to continue? The Judaism of their grandparents can no longer exist. The shared language, culture, and community of the immigrant experience is several generations behind young North American Jews. As the years march on, the Holocaust and the founding of the State of Israel, which bound Jews together in mourning and in celebration, disappear from memory and become history. What is taught about Judaism in most Hebrew schools is uninspiring, at best. In the vast majority of cases there is little Judaism in the home and no one to explain to Jewish children why they take the extra classes, away from many of their friends. For most young Jews, the strongest connection to Judaism is through family celebrations, but connection to family does not always extend to a sense of responsibility for the larger family of the Jewish people, a feeling that their grandparents possessed without question. The threat of Jewish disappearance, so alarming to me, is not enough in itself to persuade young Jews today to make Jewish choices, to build Jewish homes, and to raise Jewish children. If we want young Jews to choose Judaism, we must help them to understand what that choice means.

One thing is perfectly clear: The only way Judaism will survive in the Diaspora is through Jewish education. North American Jews, so sophisticated in all areas but their own heritage, must learn something about Judaism. Many of North America's Jewish institutions were built with the goals of finding acceptance in the larger society and fighting anti-Semitism. Now, at the opening of the twenty-first century, Jewish education must be our new mission. We must help Jews, young and old, to build a sense of connection to the Jewish people. We must help them to understand the joy that can be found in Judaism, and remind them that in the midst of joy we cannot forget those in pain. We must impart some knowledge of the texts and history of our tradition. We must show, through education and example, the value and relevance of Jewish ethics.

It all gets back to Jewish pride. To me, there is something very satisfying in knowing who I am and where I come from. By asserting my Jewishness, I am keeping faith with my ancestors and being true to myself. I am proud of the fact that Jews gave the Ten Commandments to the world. I am proud of the Talmud, that body of Biblical interpretation that contains our ethics and so much more. I like the fact that we each have a direct relationship to the Almighty and our rabbis are here to teach, not to forgive our sins. Only God can do that; hence we ourselves are responsible for our actions. I love the Jewish mystical concept of *tikkun olam,* repair of the world, based on the idea that man is God's partner in creation. Our tradition teaches that we must not only take care of the world but also improve it.

To realize what Jews have contributed to civilization is a

giant step on the road to understanding what we as Jews stand for. In every field we have excelled. Why? Because our tradition makes us ask questions. Persecution has only made us work harder to succeed. It isn't any accident that the Israel Philharmonic Orchestra has the best string section in the world—it's full of Russian Jews who are superb musicians. It's no accident that the best doctors in the world are Jews. But it's not enough for young Jews to revel in the accomplishments of other Jews. They must also have some understanding of what Judaism means. Pride without knowledge is empty and won't last. You can't be truly proud of something you know nothing about.

I asked Rabbi David Hartman if there had ever been a time and place in Jewish history when all Jews were educated about Judaism, and he replied, "No." A call for renaissance is a call for rebirth, not for a restoration of an earlier age or a continuation of what we were doing before. Jewish renaissance must challenge the Jewish community to see where outdated ideas and structures must be discarded and our Jewish story created anew. We must use our unprecedented security and success in North America to cultivate a new kind of Jewish life, one that can flourish with freedom. We need a new flowering of a Judaism based on knowledge and pride, a Judaism of hope, not fear.

When I first took on the presidency of the World Jewish Congress, the great Rabbi Joseph Ber Soleveitchik told me, "Jews were not put here just to fight anti-Semitism." His words resonate even more deeply for me today. For centuries, Jews have fought heroically to defend other Jews, and we must continue to do so. Anti-Semitism remains a global threat that has taken new forms with the rise of Islamic fundamentalism. But the Jewish people have not stayed alive for so many years only to fight, and fighting alone will not sustain us for the future.

What do we need to ensure that Judaism not only survives, but thrives? In 1990, the late Rabbi Isidore Twersky wrote a statement that called for galvanizing change in Jewish education. His words beautifully express a vision for Jewish renaissance:

> *Our goal should be to make it possible for every Jewish person, child or adult, to be exposed to the mystery and romance of Jewish history, to the enthralling insights and special sensitivities of Jewish thought, to the sanctity and symbolism of Jewish existence, and to the power and profundity of Jewish faith.*[2]

To achieve this goal will be to reach a true golden age for North American Jewry.

Chapter 2

ABRAHAM AND SARAH'S TENT: RETHINKING INTERMARRIAGE

The task of building a significant Jewish future requires a newly hopeful attitude. Fear of assimilation and intermarriage should not replace fear of anti-Semitism. Some describe the declining numbers of Jews in North America as a "silent Holocaust" and call for more restrictive walls around Jewish identity and community. This is the wrong way to address the unintended consequence of our forebears' great success in this society. Does North American Jewry want to go back to the ghetto or forward into the twenty-first century with open arms and open hearts? We must open ourselves up to new ideas and new faces and be welcoming to all who choose to participate. Openness may not be the easiest way, but it is our only way.

It is also a strong force within our tradition. Long before the Torah commanded us to love the stranger, our forebears Abraham and Sarah practiced that dictum. In Genesis, chapter 18, we are told that after Abraham's self-inflicted circumcision "[t]he Lord appeared to him by the terebinths of Mamre; he was sitting at the entrance of the tent as the day grew hot." Strikingly, Abraham then seems to leave God's presence to greet three strangers:

> *Looking up, he saw three men standing near him. As soon as he saw them, he ran from the entrance of the tent to greet them and, bowing to the ground, he said, "My lords, if it please you, do not go on past your servant. Let a little water be brought; bathe your feet and recline under the tree. And let me fetch you a morsel of bread that you may refresh yourselves; then go on—seeing that you have come your servant's way."*

How do we understand these lines? Jewish tradition teaches us to read closely and to explore all possible interpretations. This allows us to discover the ethical wisdom, both overt and subtle, in the foundational stories of the Jewish people. So, one could understand the passage in two ways: It could be saying that God has appeared *through* the three men or that the appearance of the three strangers is separate from the appearance of God.

If we interpret the lines in the second way, they make a dramatic statement: Welcoming guests is so important to Abraham that he even interrupts God to greet them. The strangers, Abraham soon learns, are angels who foretell Sarah's pregnancy, as well as the destruction of Sodom and Gomorrah; but he does not know this when he invites them in to bathe their feet and take refreshment. It would seem that greeting any weary travelers and giving them relief from the heat of the desert sun is enough to draw him away even from the presence of God.

The rabbis of the Talmud, the compilation of oral traditions that interpret the Bible, expand upon this latter interpretation. I am fascinated with the close relationship our sages found between welcoming the stranger and honoring God. Rabbi Yehuda, in the name of the Rav, learns from the Genesis text that "[w]elcoming guests is greater than receiving the Divine Presence." A later text by a medieval commentator, the Maharal, Rabbi Yehuda Loew of Prague, draws on the idea that all human beings are created in the image of God to conclude that "[w]hen you welcome a guest it is tantamount to honoring God."[1]

Indeed, the Talmud describes Abraham and Sarah as exemplars of hospitality. One midrash (rabbinic interpretation) teaches that Abraham's tent was open on all four sides so that he could welcome travelers approaching from all directions.[2] Another tells us: "All the years that Sarah was alive . . . the doors of the tent were wide open. . . . There was blessing in the dough of the bread. . . . There was a light burning from one Shabbat eve to the next Shabbat eve."[3]

The meaning is clear. You can bathe yourself in the spirit of God, but more important is to honor your fellow human beings. One of the reasons I love being a Jew is that we value moral action over religious belief. How we treat the stranger is one of the greatest measures of that value. Our behavior toward newcomers to Judaism should reflect the spirit of welcome in the Jewish tradition.

As we foster a renaissance in Jewish life today, we must ask what kind of Jewish community we want to create. I cannot say exactly what all Jews should learn or how they should practice their Judaism—the pathway to Jewish knowledge and pride is not the same for everyone, and different people will experience it in their different ways. But I do know that if we are to create a vital Judaism for our time, we must do more than preserve and protect what we have. Like Judaism at its Biblical beginnings, the Judaism of the future should be open and hospitable, not closed and fearful. We need to cultivate the hopeful attitude that if we embrace it, our religion is strong enough to sustain the new ideas and new faces of the twenty-first century.

Let us remember Abraham and Sarah's tent as we confront the high rates of intermarriage in North America. It is terribly important that Abraham doesn't even ask the three strangers who they are or where they are going. He simply accepts them. We should take the same approach to intermarried Jews and their families, whether or not the non-Jewish members should choose to convert. In an open society, people from diverse backgrounds will fall in love. The key question is whether or not intermarried couples will raise their children as Jews. If we speak about intermarriage as a disaster for the Jewish people, we send a message to intermarried families that is mixed at best. How can you welcome people in while at the same time telling them that their loving relationship is in part responsible for the destruction of the Jewish people? No one should be made to feel our welcome is conditional or begrudging. The many non-Jews who marry Jews must not be regarded as a threat to Jewish survival but as honored guests in a house of joy, learning, and pride.

I spoke about intermarriage with Rabbi David Ellenson, whose attitude toward the issue resonated with me. Ellenson is president of HUC–JIR, Reform Judaism's academic and professional development center, with branches in Los Angeles, Cincinnati, New York, and Israel. He is an extraordinary man and a Jew of the future. In the North American Jewish community, we need to cultivate both respect for Jewish tradition and openness to the needs of our diverse Jewish population, and Ellenson is a leader who richly possesses both. He has a Ph.D. in modern Jewish history and sociology and has published extensively on diverse topics in Jewish history, ethics, and thought. A leader of the Reform Movement, he is the product of Orthodox parents and a strict Orthodox home, and his personal habits still reflect his upbringing: He often wears a *kippah,* and he obeys kashrut. As a person and as a Jewish leader, he is the epitome of welcoming, a man who is wide open to the Biblical rule of loving the stranger.

Ellenson underscored the prevalence of intermarriage in Jewish life today. He pointed out that with about half of Jews marrying non-Jews, it means that, without taking conversion into account, two-thirds of our families will be intermarried. (If two out of four Jews marry each other and two marry non-Jews, the result is that two out of the three couples are intermarried.) That's what Jewish life in the United States and Canada looks like today, and we have to accept it. "I'm definitely opposed to this notion of constantly complaining and carping about what is already a reality," Ellenson told me. "It's a little bit like the Talmudic debate: Is it good that we were born? It's an interesting debate philosophically, but rather irrelevant once you're here."

Intermarriage is often blamed for the decline in Judaism and in the Jewish population in North America. But the problem is not that Jews are falling in love with non-Jews but that they aren't falling in love with Judaism.

Ellenson articulated the question we should be asking: "Given the reality of intermarriage, how does the Jewish community make Judaism an ongoing, viable alternative for people who have made this choice in their life?" He quoted Rabbi Mordecai Kaplan, who wrote in 1934 that intermarriage offered the real test of the strength of Jewish civilization, by making us ask if the Jewish community and Jewish tradition can be attractive enough that the couple, conversion aside, would ultimately choose to cast its lot with the Jewish people. The real concern is not how we deal with intermarriage but how we create a Jewish community that is compelling enough and welcoming enough to make people commit to it.

Statistics don't tell the whole story. The oft-cited figure that among intermarried families only 33 percent of children are raised Jewish[4] does not take into account the possibility that if the Jewish community were more welcoming, those numbers could grow dramatically. Intermarriage doesn't automatically mean "I'm no longer a Jew." It's more than possible to gain a Jew and, more important, another generation of

Jewish children. But this cannot happen if the Jewish partner has no Jewish knowledge or interest or the Jewish community sets up a barrier against welcoming the potential newcomer.

Ellenson went on to describe statistical matters as "self-fulfilling prophecies": "If you *shrei gevalt* over the fact that people have intermarried, and you tell people it's a disaster, and you rip your coat and all of that, it is unlikely that people will remain in the community. If, on the other hand, you embrace people, you catch more flies with honey than with vinegar." The message that we send to intermarried families must simply be "welcome."

Jewish parents have to understand that intermarriage no longer means "marrying out." If their children marry non-Jews, it's not a rebellion against them or the upbringing they gave their children. I remember one interview with a group of very Jewishly turned on students who, when I asked them if it was important to them to marry Jews, answered, universally, that it would be nice if they married Jews, but that falling in love was not something they could control. In such an open society as we now have, and with poll after poll telling us that the non-Jew is happy to marry a Jew, we cannot expect our youth to be otherwise than the way they are. The only way to keep our children absolutely Jewish and marrying only other Jews is to go back to the ghetto. I don't think North American Jewry wants that. So if we want to live in this wonderful society, we will have to rethink our taboos and face the facts. There is a lot of interfaith marriage. It isn't going away, and we have to deal with it. The Jewish community should stop talking about preventing intermarriage and start talking about teaching Judaism.

While earlier in the century intermarriage usually meant shedding Jewish identity, intermarriage today can be an opportunity to embrace it more strongly. A recent study by Brown University historian Dr. Keren McGinity examines this phenomenon for Jewish women. As her Hebrew first name and Irish last name suggest, McGinity is herself intermarried. In her study, she interviewed forty-two Jewish women of Ashkenazi (Eastern European) descent who lived in the Boston area and came from Reform, Conservative, or Orthodox backgrounds and who, between the years of 1938 and 2000, had married a non-Jew. Comparing the comments of women who had married in the earlier part of the twentieth century with those who married in the later decades, she found that while women who intermarried earlier had abandoned their Jewish traditions and practices along with their Jewish last names, for the younger women intermarrying often catalyzed a new embrace of Judaism. McGinity explains this shift as a result of the societal changes in the 1960s and 1970s: the lowering of racial and ethnic barriers, the feminist movement, and the rise of interest in ethnicity. Women felt the freedom both to marry out of their faith and to insist on carrying it on. The admitted challenge of doing so in a mixed marriage made them learn more about Judaism. One woman interviewed said, "I am carrying more weight around here and with my family, because my husband is looking to me on different holidays to show the way. So maybe that has made me stiffen my back a bit and do some reading and learn how to carry the show, like maybe I wouldn't have to if I'd married someone else who is Jewish."[5]

The Jewish community should be working to support and encourage intermarried Jews like the woman quoted here, not condemning intermarriage. If we are welcoming and offer Jewish educational opportunities for all, it is likely that more and more intermarried couples will opt to raise their children as Jews.

One leader working toward this goal is Rabbi Kerry M. Olitzky, executive director of the Jewish Outreach Institute (JOI) in New York City. JOI was founded in 1988, primarily as a think tank and research institute at City University, to study the then-growing phenomenon of intermarriage. JOI continues to do research, but currently its primary mission is to create a more inclusive Jewish community, particularly for interfaith families.

"What we want to do is change the agenda from talking about interfaith marriage to talking about raising Jewish children," Olitzky told me in our interview. "Even if you can do something about the future [rates] of intermarriage, you still have to grapple with the million-plus families that you have."

Olitzky distinguished between three kinds of intermarriages. On one end are couples raising Jewish children, and on the other end are those raising Christian children. Then there is a large group in the middle, whose children are being raised in what he called the "American civil religion." In these homes,

"Fourth of July and Thanksgiving become much more important than Rosh Hashanah, Yom Kippur, Passover, and Chanukah. You will often find a Chanukah menorah as well as a
Christmas tree, an Easter basket as well as a Passover seder."
Olitzky sees potential for Jewish connection in these essentially secular families: "As soon as the organized Jewish
community sees a Christmas tree or something similar, they
write off that family. That's the biggest mistake that can be
made. Would I prefer they didn't have one? Yes. But I'm still
prepared to deal with the family even if they do." I strongly
agree. We should make the effort to reach out to all families,
and instead of chastising them for their choices, we should
try to show them the value in Jewish tradition.

JOI recently sponsored a study of adult children of intermarriage, in which ninety young adults completed a face-to-
face interview and a brief survey. The study found that while
many of these young adults have had little Jewish education,
most see Judaism as important and want to "transmit a Jewish ethnic identity to their children." Yet only a small minority has had significant contact with Jewish institutional life,
as in synagogues or Jewish Community Centers.

For Olitzky, the survey's findings "suggest that the door to
Jewish life among the children of intermarriage may still be
open, but in most cases the Jewish community has yet to
come knocking." A concerted effort must be made to reach
them, "because many have experienced (or anticipate) rejection from the community." The Jewish community must
reach out to "ignite the dormant Jewish sparks."[6]

How can this be accomplished? Olitzky has several answers: "Jewish culture, rather than religion, is the more logical doorway in." Also, "more programming should take place outside the physical confines of Jewish establishments, because the vast majority of these children—like their intermarried parents—are simply not walking through the doors of our institutions." He would also like to see Jewish education brought directly into the home, where educators could work with entire families: "The easiest way to start is the family celebration of holidays, because that's the way children can relate and that's the way families relate. I would want to bring the joyful experience of Judaism into the home."

Olitzky told me that many in the organized Jewish community are beginning to recognize that they have to reach out to intermarried families: "I think our work is finally getting on the radar screens of major and minor Jewish communities and organizations. But it's an uphill battle." Those who speak in the name of the Jewish community really represent its minority, not its majority. Communal leaders have to get in step with the realities of North American Jewish life. "Federations are beginning to understand that there's a ripple effect with regard to its donor base. They will not be able to raise funds from a community they're not serving."

For large segments of the Jewish community, resistance to dealing with intermarried families comes from the issue of how we define a Jew. The question of who is a Jew has caused great controversy in the Jewish community. The Reform and Reconstructionist movements will consider you

Jewish if you have formally converted or if either parent is a Jew and you have been raised as a Jew. In the Orthodox and Conservative movements, however, a Jew is defined as a person born to a Jewish mother or converted by an Orthodox or Conservative rabbi. Thus, if a Jewish man marries a non-Jewish woman, a portion of the Jewish community will not consider the children of the marriage Jewish, no matter how they practice or how they identify themselves.

The situation is compounded by policies in Israel. One of Israel's major problems is the monopoly that Israel's first prime minister, David Ben-Gurion, gave the Orthodox over the lives of Israeli Jews. He was as secular as one gets. However, in exchange for their political support, he granted the Orthodox control of the state's Jewish religious establishment. In his mind, the new state was going to be secular, with the new Jew as farmer, soldier, kibbutznik, and unselfish, freedom-loving paragon. Ben-Gurion thought that the religious Jews simply would not be significant. It didn't work out that way. Today, the Orthodox have a monopoly on Judaism, and Reform and Conservative weddings, funerals, and conversions performed in Israel are not recognized. To further complicate matters, Israel's Law of Return grants citizenship to any immigrant with one Jewish grandparent. Yet because of the Orthodox control over religion, an Israeli who was not born to a Jewish mother or converted by an Orthodox rabbi cannot be married to a Jew or buried in a Jewish cemetery in Israel. These wrongheaded and contradictory policies have led to the tragic situation that many Russian-immigrant soldiers who have died fighting for Israel are forbidden burial in a Jewish cemetery because their mothers were not Jewish.

Rabbi Donniel Hartman, codirector of the Shalom Hartman Institute, led a study session at my office entitled "Who are the Jews?" He began by explaining that without the "glue" of anti-Semitism that helped define our sense of peoplehood, our community is breaking down into antagonistic groups, as Jews of different denominations refuse to recognize each other as Jews. That we not only advocate competing and conflicting notions of Judaism but also disagree as to who even is a Jew is a threat to our survival as a people. He asserted that we need a kind of "shared membership policy" by which all can agree on who counts as a Jew.

Hartman led us through classic sources to investigate how such a policy might be adapted to our times. From the Biblical through the contemporary era, he explained, there have been three ways to become Jewish. The first is through birth, as with God's words to Abraham in Genesis: "I will make of thee a great nation. . . . To thy seed I will give this land."[7] In the Bible, it was being born to a Jewish father that mattered: Jacob had twelve sons and one daughter, and four different women were the mothers. Two, the Torah tells us, were wives, as well as each other's sisters, and the other two were concubines. We have no idea of their religions or tribal backgrounds. For reasons that are the subject of debate, the rabbis of the Talmud changed the law to matrilineal descent: When only one of the parents is Jewish, it is the mother's religion that determines membership.

That Jewish identity comes with birth is deeply ingrained in Jewish life, Hartman commented, and it is both a strength and a danger. On the one hand, the idea of Judaism as an ethnicity has offered a basis for Jewish "collective moral responsibility" and inspired Jews to help other Jews around the world, from Russia to Israel to Ethiopia. On the other hand, ethnic loyalty can become ethnocentrism, blinding us to the humanity of others.

The second way to become Jewish has been through cultural assimilation through intermarriage. As Hartman writes, this was present in the Biblical period prior to the sixth century B.C.E., when it was deemed illegal by Ezra. Prior to Ezra, "Bnei Yisrael [the Children of Israel] were not constituted by men and women of Israelite descent alone, but often by Israelite men and non-Israelite women who married into the community." The first examples of this are "when the matriarchs and the subsequent wives of the sons of Jacob are integrated as members, despite their non Abrahamic ancestry." All forms of intermarriage, however, were not permitted. Hartman shows that intermarriage was forbidden in cases where the religion of the spouse is likely to dominate: "For they will turn your children away from Me to worship other gods."[8] It is only when the religion of the family was likely to be Jewish that intermarriage was sanctioned and offered an entry point to membership in the Jewish community.

During the rabbinic period, the rabbis added the ritual of conversion as a process for becoming part of the Jewish community. From a legal perspective, conversion has continued through the modern times as the only alternative to being born to a Jewish mother. However, today many non-Jews in North America who are married to Jews are affiliating with the Jewish people, even if they have not converted themselves. The same situation applies to Russian immigrants in Israel. Hartman explains that this has meant intermarriage is once again a de facto way of "acquiring membership" in the Jewish community.

Today, the denominations have deep disagreements over each of the "classic features of the Jewish membership policy," from what rituals constitute a conversion to patrilineal versus matrilineal descent. For the sake of keeping our peoplehood alive, Hartman argues for the following "functional solution": The Jewish community as a whole ought to adopt a policy that "membership" in the Jewish people may be determined by any of the past membership policies, be it birth by patrilineal or matrilineal descent, conversion by any denomination, or cultural assimilation through intermarriage. The denominations need not agree over who counts as a Jew according to Jewish law, he argues, but they should agree that in almost all cases where membership rights count, such as membership in a Jewish organization or citizenship in the State of Israel, there is no reason to adopt a limited and mutually discriminating policy. Marriage is the only area that would require a consensus on Jewish law (i.e., if an Orthodox and patrilineally descended Jew wish to be married by an Orthodox rabbi), but there, too, he argues, functional solutions can be found. While he recognizes the difficulty of adopting such a mutually inclusive policy, he makes an impassioned call that for the sake of the Jewish people, we need to think beyond the narrow interests of the denominations. "The threat to our collective life is real and it is our religious responsibility to respond," he writes.[9]

Hartman's ideas make a lot of sense to me. That the Jewish community continues to fight about who is a Jew is self-defeating. We have to put aside our differences and agree that, for the good of the Jewish people, we must open our doors and invite Jewish connection for all who wish to enter. If patrilineally descended Jews choose to affiliate with an Orthodox Jewish community, they can convert. But a focus on this issue will only turn other Jews and potential Jews away from Jewish life. Our concern as a community now should be to welcome people into our community, not to build boundaries around it. Conversion should be a choice people make from their hearts and when they are ready, not a condition by which they and their children are accepted into the Jewish community. There are many non-Jews who may not be ready to formally convert—particularly if their parents are living—but may be willing to raise their children as Jews.

From my son Adam I learned how insulting it is if your children, who have a non-Jewish mother, are considered not to be Jews by other Jews, despite the fact that they grew up in a Jewish home and were more Jewishly educated than so many children of inmarried people. Adam, who works alongside me in furthering the Jewish renaissance at The Samuel

Bronfman Foundation, married "out" some twenty years ago. Cindy, his wonderful wife, was born Catholic, and together they decided to raise their children in a Jewish home. They observe Shabbat every week, lighting candles, blessing the children, and studying Torah. The children have grown up with a strong sense of their Jewish identity and a strong foundation of knowledge about their traditions and culture. Cindy chose to convert to Judaism in 2006, but that decision is highly personal and should not be the crucial factor in determining whether or not children raised as Jews in a proudly Jewish home should be considered Jewish by the community. Like Adam, who is a committed Reform Jew, I strongly agree that patrilineal descent should be accepted throughout the Jewish community.

David Ellenson explained his own perspective as follows: If you know that historical factors led to the creation of matrilineal descent, "[w]hy would you not allow other historical factors to alter the way you would view this tradition?" In his view, "persons who are raised Jewishly, identify themselves Jewishly, are committed Jewishly" should be considered to be Jewish. He quoted David Ben-Gurion, who once defined a Jew as anyone who calls himself a Jew and isn't anything else.

What's more, Ellenson added, "[w]hat would be the most that we'd be guilty of" if we embraced people who might not technically be Jewish according to *halachah,* or Jewish law? "That we loved too much? We need a community where more and more of our leaders love Jews as much as they love Judaism."

Non-Jewish spouses who raise their children as Jewish should be welcomed unconditionally, even while those who do convert should be celebrated. "I would like it if people make that choice," Ellenson said. But the question, he continued, is not how we get people to convert but how we bring them into the community and teach whole families about Judaism: "I think of the countless numbers of non-Jewish parents, non-Jewish spouses, who bring their children to religious school, to Hebrew school, who see to it that they have bar- and bat-mitzvah lessons, who put the money forth for their children to go to day schools, etc. These are people who should be embraced by our community. Some of them, maybe, will ultimately also convert."

Those non-Jews who have committed themselves to raising their children as Jews have made what for many is a difficult choice, and they should be honored for that choice. One of the most moving documents I have read on the subject is "Blessing for Non-Jewish Spouses," delivered to a packed synagogue on Yom Kippur morning by Rabbi Janet Marder of Congregation Beth Am in Los Altos Hills, California. This blessing left the whole synagogue in tears, and it has the same effect when you read it cold on the computer screen, and not just the first time. It beautifully expresses the spirit of welcome that must suffuse the entire Jewish community. Her introduction to it is included here:

Today I want to recognize and publicly acknowledge for the first time some very important people in our congregation. They are part of Beth Am because, somewhere along the way, they happened to fall in love with a Jewish man or woman, and that decision changed their life. I want to let you know in advance that in a few moments I am going to be calling up all non-Jewish spouses to come to the bima for a special blessing of thanks and appreciation.

I hope that you will not be embarrassed or upset that I am singling you out in this way. The last thing I want is to make you feel uncomfortable. What I do want is to tell you how much you matter to our congregation, and how very grateful we are for what you have done.

You are a very diverse group of people. Some of you are living a Jewish life in virtually all respects. Some of you are devoutly committed to another faith. Some of you do not define yourselves as religious at all. You fall at all points along this spectrum, and we acknowledge and respect your diversity.

What we want to thank you for today is your decision to cast your lot with the Jewish people by becoming part of this congregation, and the love and support you give to your Jewish partner. Most of all, we want to offer our deepest thanks to those of you who are parents, and who are raising your sons and daughters as Jews.

In our generation, which saw one-third of the world's Jewish population destroyed, every Jewish child is especially precious. We are a very small people, and history has made us smaller. Our children mean hope, and they mean life. So every Jewish boy and girl is a gift to the Jewish future. With all our hearts, we want to thank you for your generosity and strength of spirit in making the ultimate gift to the Jewish people.

Please, please . . . do not be shy and do not feel uncomfortable. It is important that we show you how much you have our love and

ABRAHAM AND SARAH'S TENT

respect, and there is no better time to say that than on the most important day in the Jewish year. Please come up now, and receive the heartfelt gratitude of your congregation.[10]

As we face a troubled world and a shrinking Jewish community, we must ask ourselves what it means to truly become a Jew. Instead of arguing about inclusion and exclusion, let us embrace the Jewish ethic of caring for our fellow human beings. The most beautiful example of this is in the Book of Ruth. During a time of famine in the land of Israel, Naomi comes to the land of Moab with her two sons, who both marry local women. After the death of her husband and both sons, Naomi decides to return to Israel. A destitute widow, she tells her two daughters-in-law to return to their families and their gods. One complies, but the other, Ruth, speaks the beautiful words that wed her to her mother-in-law's religion: "Do not urge me to leave you, to turn back and not follow you. For wherever you go, I will go; wherever you lodge, I will lodge; your people shall be my people, and your God my God."[11]

For the rabbis of the Talmud, Ruth is the first convert, and her story is the source of present-day conversion rituals. There is even a midrash that states that Naomi taught Ruth all the laws and prohibitions attached to Judaism. But the Biblical text says nothing about rules that Ruth must learn in order to become a Jew. Rather, Ruth becomes a Jew through her extraordinary act of *chesed,* or kindness. We should remember this story as we face the conflicts of today. Ruth is the ultimate outsider: She is a Moabite, a tribe with whom intermarriage is specifically forbidden in the Bible. Yet in her great act of loyalty to her mother-in-law Ruth not only becomes a Jew but also makes possible the redemption of the Jewish people, as the ancestress of King David. What do we keep out as we exclude those who would join our Jewish community? Perhaps it is by embracing the outsider that we will ultimately bring our community, and our world, the leaders we most need.[12]

Chapter 3

A NEW JUDAISM FOR A NEW GENERATION: ENGAGING THE DISENGAGED

Reaching In to Reach Out

It's not only intermarried families that need a warm welcome. Today, more Jews than ever before are disconnected from Jewish life. Some say that we should commit our resources to those who are already engaged with Judaism and let the others fall away. This idea is a disservice to the strength of our tradition and to the creativity that those who are not considered "insiders" can bring to the table. What's more, the process of reaching out benefits everyone. By trying to convey the importance of Judaism to the many Jews who are not involved in Jewish life, "insiders" reach in to explore why Judaism really matters and become more involved, educated Jews.

When I started writing this book, I wasn't as aware as I am now of the importance of outreach. Not only can we stop the outflow of Jews, but we also can even increase our numbers if we behave rationally. Fostering a Judaism that appeals to many Jews in North America means fostering a Judaism that is relevant for our time. It means reaching out so that all Jews can learn something about Judaism and can add their own voices to the larger conversation.

David Ellenson described the situation as follows. "We have two trends in American Judaism," he told me. On the one hand, "the core of people who are committed Jewishly is probably stronger than ever. So that in part, we can boast of the renaissance in Jewish life.... Where Judaism is healthy, it's unbelievably healthy. Simultaneously we have more people who are unaffiliated than ever before, because the factors that led people of my generation and my parents' generation to affiliate Jewishly are no longer there."

Ellenson articulated his strong belief that Judaism offers something much needed in today's world, where the array of choices leaves many feeling disconnected. If Judaism is welcoming, Ellenson said, it can help people to feel a sense of meaning in their lives, leading more Jews to become active in Jewish life and more intermarried families to raise their children as Jews. As one step, Ellenson called for more classes "for born Jews and born non-Jews alike who come within our ambit or orbit, to introduce them to the customs and traditions of our people." This kind of education must "be done in a loving way that ultimately demonstrates that Jewish religious tradition will one day be relevant for how they construct their own lives."

The Reform Movement has been an innovative leader of

outreach in Jewish life, and other movements should learn from its efforts. The watershed moment came in 1978 with a statement by Rabbi Alexander Schindler, then president of the synagogue arm of the Reform Movement, the Union of American Hebrew Congregations (UAHC), which is now known as the Union for Reform Judaism (URJ). In an address to the UAHC board of trustees, Schindler responded to rapidly increasing rates of intermarriage with a call for active welcome to "Jews by choice" and to interfaith families. He also called for programs to reach "unchurched" seekers of "religious meaning."[1]

In the decades that followed, the URJ developed a program of outreach designed to reach both unaffiliated Jews and non-Jews. I spoke about these efforts with Dru Greenwood, who for more than ten years was head of outreach for the URJ. I wanted to hear from a practitioner of outreach, who is a convert herself, about what draws people to Judaism and how the Jewish community can effectively welcome them. "My sense is that there are people who can find a home in Judaism, and who in fact are looking for a home in Judaism, who just need the door opened," Greenwood told me.

I asked Greenwood just what about Judaism resonated with her. She spoke about the "tremendous hope" in the story of the Exodus from Egypt, the foundational narrative that Jewish prayers continually tell us to remember. The story teaches, Greenwood said, that God brings people from "narrow, constricted places to live fully ethical lives, to help repair the world, to be partners with God." She spoke about the direct relationship with God and the beauty she felt in the holiday cycle.

Greenwood's path as an outreach professional began with her own conversion to Judaism in 1970, the same year she married her Jewish husband. "Did you convert because of marriage?" I asked.

"I think that my conversion was catalyzed by our relationship, because that's how I found out about Judaism," she said. "His Judaism was very important to him, and I was very interested in it. We went and took an Introduction to Judaism class even before we were engaged. As we were sitting there in that class, bells were going off for me. I felt like I was coming home to something."

At the time she converted, Greenwood said, people didn't talk openly about intermarriage and conversion. She explained that the silence around conversion was meant to protect people from embarrassment, but it made it difficult for converts to become integrated into the Jewish community. You have a close relationship with a rabbi while you're learning, she pointed out, and then you have a dunk in the *mikvah* (the ritual bath) and you're on your own. Having been through the process herself, she recognized that people must be able to give voice to their questions and experiences and to know that they're not alone.

Greenwood became involved in early efforts to integrate new converts into the synagogue community at Boston's Temple Israel and went on to work for the URJ's national office. She helped to create programs aimed at interfaith couples and potential converts and described the tremendous gratitude she felt as people began to talk about subjects that had previously been taboo.

Then, in 1989, she and her colleagues began to realize that Jews need outreach as much or perhaps more than non Jews: "We were doing a lot of work for interfaith couples and for people who wanted to come into Judaism, but we weren't reaching out to unaffiliated Jews." So, with Greenwood's leadership, the URJ started a program called A Taste of Judaism: Are You Curious? aimed at intermarried couples, non-Jewish seekers, and Jews who did not belong to a synagogue. Advertised in the secular press, it is a three-session course of two hours each that invites participants to "[c]ome explore Jewish spirituality, Jewish ethics, Jewish community." A survey of the first 2,000 participants reported that 33 percent had gone on to take the Introduction to Judaism course, 14 percent of the non-Jews were interested in conversion, and 28 percent of the Jews had joined synagogues. Now there have been 60,000 people who have gone through the exercise.

Greenwood explained the overlapping needs of non-Jews and Jews and the synergy that developed between the two populations: "Unaffiliated Jews would come in with lots of baggage," as if they were "giving this one last try." The non-Jews who sat next to them came in "asking all of these naïve questions" that were in fact the same questions the unaffiliated Jews wanted to ask: Is there a God? Is there a place for me? What does it mean to be a good Jew? As the rabbi responded, Greenwood said, she could see the Jews in the class "sitting up straighter and straighter, and taking pride." She added, amusingly, that food is necessary at these meetings—as Abraham and Sarah knew, it's the number one outreach tool.

Greenwood makes a compelling case that there is a hunger and that people can be reached. Dru Greenwood looked at Judaism and liked what she saw and now makes it her life's work to invite as many as she can to join with her.

While the Reform Movement has been at the forefront of outreach efforts, there are leaders across the denominations who have made it their mission to bring the beauty and meaning of Judaism to a broad audience. Rabbi Harold Schulweis, in Los Angeles, is one of these leaders. Schulweis possesses a profound love of the Jewish people and a vision for the Jewish community that reaches across denominational boundaries. Born in the Bronx in a secular Zionist household, he was influenced by his grandfather, an immigrant from the shtetl who studied Talmud all day, and chose to attend a yeshiva high school and, later, Yeshiva University. Drawn to the teaching of Abraham Joshua Heschel and Mordecai Kaplan, he received his rabbinic ordination at the Jewish Theological Seminary. He moved to California, where he found the atmosphere freer for innovation. In his long career as a rabbi, Schulweis has been the leader of many innovative efforts, including bringing the *havurah* movement into the synagogue.

One of the teachings that drew me to Schulweis was the following quotation: "In order to have outreach, you have to have inreach." He makes a very convincing case that inreach and outreach go together. Those who are already involved in Jewish life can best learn about the spirit and content of Judaism by teaching others and by welcoming them into their homes. And outreach will only be truly effective if it comes from deep within an understanding mind and an open heart.

Despite what he called the Conservative Movement's "standoffish" approach to outreach, Schulweis began a program at his synagogue designed to connect with "un-churched Christians and un-synagogued Jews." A small advertisement in the *Los Angeles Times*, which began with "Searching," brought two hundred people for each of fifteen Wednesday night lectures. The non-Jews who came were not motivated by marriage, Schulweis said: "These people were genuinely interested in the ethical wisdom of Judaism, and its civilizational character."

Schulweis's concept of "inreach through outreach" arose when he asked his congregants to welcome the converts who came through the lecture program: "I said to my people, born Jews, 'I'd like you to open your homes, I'd like you to invite them to a Shabbat.'" Their response surprised him: "They said, 'I don't know how to do Shabbos.' I said, 'What do you mean?' They said, 'I don't know what comes first, the kiddush [blessing over wine] or the candles or *hamotzi* [blessing over bread]?' I said, 'Wonderful. Now you have a purpose—you'll learn a great deal.'"

In a sermon to his congregants, Schulweis made an urgent plea for compliance with his vision. He asked his congregants,

"Will you volunteer to 'reach in' so that we can 'reach out' to potential Jews?" He urged them to embark on a program of study so that they could become mentoring teachers to those who are new to Judaism. The purpose, he stated, is "to study so that you can teach. To teach so that you can persuade. To persuade so that you can transmit the ethics, the spirit, the culture of a four-thousand-year tradition."[2]

Schulweis spoke to me about the beauty of teaching and learning at the same time. I know what he means. When I teach Torah to my grandchildren, I have to study the material before I present it to them. I told my eight-year-old grandson that the relation between the two of us really isn't as teacher and pupil. That's for school. What we are doing is studying together, which is a very Jewish concept. The more we talk, the more he questions. To answer his questions, I often have to look deeper into the texts and further my own knowledge. Reaching out, especially to those in your own family, means challenging yourself to explore what Judaism means to you and taking responsibility for conveying your love of Judaism to others. I do not pray that my grandchildren will be Jewish, though I dearly hope they will choose that path. I pray for the resolve, patience, and wisdom to be able to teach them, if I can, about Judaism. In provoking them to ask questions about the Biblical texts we read together, I build a relationship that I hope will help them to lead good lives, I hope as Jews, but even if not, at least as adults who have some knowledge of Judaism and warm memories of their grandfather.

Schulweis described what Judaism offers to those who have difficulty with the concept of God. His emphasis is always on Judaism's ethical teachings and its focus on how you live your life. In his book *For Those Who Can't Believe*, Schulweis writes about the way we can believe in "Godliness" as being good, even if we cannot believe in God.[3] "I'm talking about a quality of life that you believe in, that you perpetuate, that you teach to your children and to your people," he told me. "That's called Elohut, or Godliness."

It is the ethical dimension of Judaism that should be taught across the community, Schulweis told me. He is critical of any teaching that leaves out the "why": "We always think that Judaism is simply law and obedience. It's what my grandfather taught me; it's what the yeshiva taught; it's what the seminary taught. But the point is there's a vast literature in Judaism that is religious audacity, in which God is challenged, and in which, through these challenges, laws are changed."

As an example, he asked if I knew why the mezuzah is placed at an angle instead of vertically or horizontally. He explained as follows. In the Bible, we are told: "You shall teach these commandments unto your children, when you rise up, when you lie down." The commentator Rashi said that since it says "rise up," it should be done vertically. His grandson, Rashbam, said that since it says "lie down," the mezuzah should be placed horizontally. The result? They compromised. From this we can learn, Schulweis told me, that "in a home, strength is not saying, 'My way or no way.' It's compromise. Now that, to me, is an ethical teaching." He complained that teachers "never explain that, because the important thing is that it's a commandment, 'Do it and shut up!'"

Schulweis is something of a renegade in the Conservative Movement, and the further right we move on the religious spectrum, the more difficult it is to find outreach. (A notable exception is the Lubavitchers, who approach outreach with the particular agenda of bringing nonobservant Jews into their Orthodox fold. Most New York Jews are aware of the Lubavitcher mitzvah wagons that cruise the streets looking to bring what they call "lapsed Jews" back into a prayer mode. The Lubavitchers are admirable in that they will work in places in the world where no one else will go. My wife and I met a pair of Lubavitchers in Kazakhstan who had organized the Jewish community of Almaty to build a synagogue.) Still, visionary Modern Orthodox rabbis share the sense that all Jews must be invited to participate in Jewish life and that we must make an effort to reach them.

One of these visionaries is Rabbi Avi Weiss. Weiss is perhaps best known for his international political activism on behalf of the Jewish people: He has confronted former Ku Klux Klan member David Duke and Nation of Islam leader Louis Farrakhan, protested the building of a convent at Auschwitz, and fought tirelessly on behalf of Soviet Jews and the State of Israel. More recently, however, Weiss has focused his energy on education and spiritual life within the Jewish community. He is the senior rabbi and spiritual leader

of the Hebrew Institute of Riverdale, an Orthodox synagogue that has drawn in Jews from many backgrounds. He is
also the founder and president of Yeshivat Chovevei Torah,
an open Orthodox rabbinical school. While he is committed
to Orthodox Judaism, he clearly states that his goal is "to
serve all of Am Israel, the whole of the Jewish people."

I asked Weiss, "What, in your opinion, is the best way to
try to get unaffiliated or, to use my term, not self-identified
Jews to become identified Jews?"

"I think the key to reaching an unaffiliated Jew is through
love," Weiss told me. "To welcome people and to accept
them for who they are, no strings attached. I think that most
unaffiliated Jews feel that nobody cares about them." His
synagogue, he said, is called the *bayit*, which means "home": "A
home is a place of love, and we want people to feel welcome."
In the synagogue, he doesn't sit in the front but among the
people, so that he can be the first to welcome them in the
door. He described how his synagogue offers free High
Holiday services and a free Passover seder, all of which attract hundreds of people, many of whom are unaffiliated.

He continued, "The second key is to remember that there
are different ways of reaching Jews." Some Jews may be
turned off to ritual but access Judaism in other ways. In his
experience, many have entered Jewish communal life through
activism, of the kind he has been involved in as president of
AMCHA—The Coalition for Jewish Concerns: "I have met,
in my forty years of activism, probably in the thousands, literally, of Jews who knew nothing about spiritual Judaism,

who stood with me on this or that. And once they stood, if it's presented in a way that has a spiritual dimension, then it could be the point of entry to do much, much more."

I asked his view about making a Jewish home, something that is elementary to the raising of Jewish children. He described his approach as an exploration of the beauty Judaism can bring to the home and family life: "Take the Sabbath. . . . Abraham Joshua Heschel talks about how we live in a world of technical civilization. And certainly, to be successful in this world is something very important in Torah." But Heschel describes the way "acquisition of things of space" comes at the expense of time. Weiss quoted Heschel's beautiful line: "'Yet to have more does not mean to be more.'[4] Having is not being. And as I see it, six days of the week are days of having, aspiring to have. And that's noble. But for one day during the week, let's focus not on having but on being. Let's focus not so much on existence but on essence. Let's focus on: What's the purpose of this all? Why am I working for six days? So we need a sabbatical day. . . . It's that time where I can sit down with my family, without a TV, without a radio, where I'm not being acted upon, where I can interact with those who are closest to me. It's hard work. It takes a lot of energy. But it's often the case that what is hard work is most meaningful."

Weiss has a true sense of the Jewish people as a family and feels a sense of responsibility toward and love for all members of that family, however they might choose to practice. His motive for reaching out is not about making people like him; in fact, he objected to the term "outreach," since it implies that the person reaching out has the answer and the person being brought in has little to offer. "The word I prefer is 'encounter.' It's a two-way street. No matter the level of learning or observance of the individual, that person has much to bring to the table, and we have much to learn from each other. I'm not out for people to replicate my lifestyle." While he admitted "an honest bias—I think, for example, that people should keep the Sabbath," he says that his goal as an Orthodox rabbi is not to make people Orthodox but to "kindle the spark" that will help people to find their own paths.

An Open Book

Abraham's tent, as we've seen, was open on all sides. Jewish community must also be open: to new ideas, new conditions, and new models of Judaism. For centuries, Judaism has gained new life through exchange of ideas with other cultures, and we must continue in opening our book to current ideas and concerns.

It is Judaism's intrinsic openness to the outside world, even as it offers a rooted identity, that makes it particularly relevant for our society today. Rabbi David Hartman illuminated this point in my interview with him. Hartman is a leading thinker in the field of Jewish philosophy and an internationally renowned author. He lives in Jerusalem and is, as mentioned earlier, founder and codirector of the Shalom Hartman Institute, where religiously diverse Jewish scholars gather to study Jewish sources and issues in contemporary Jewish life.

With emancipation and the breaking down of ghetto walls in the modern world, Hartman told me, the major issue that modern Jews have faced is: Can they integrate their deep roots in their own tradition with an openness to the larger world? Hartman's answer is a passionate yes: "The biggest problem that all moderns feel is anomie, the lack of relationship, the lack of passion. And they're looking for ways in which they can relocate their identity. Therefore Jews developed particularity and, at the same time, our openness to the world at large." To embrace Judaism is to build "an identity through strong roots and through attachment, instead of just floating freely in the world. . . . Judaism always insisted on the importance of relationship, in the family, in the community. And out of that strong relational framework, you then go out to the larger world."

Hartman celebrates Judaism's essential relationship with the wider world of learning, peoples, and cultures: "Being a Jew doesn't mean that I have to close my eyes to what is beautiful in the world. Nothing that's human should be strange to a Jew. That's my deepest motto. The Book of Genesis doesn't begin with a God who is Jewish. God is the creation of all life. He becomes Jewish when he meets Abraham. And therefore he moves from the universal to the particular. But the particular and the universal always fundamentally were joined together. I want the particular to enrich the universal, and I want the universal to enrich the particular."

I asked, "But didn't Torah originally mean us to be separate and to be different?"

"Only if the world is corrupt," Hartman said. "If the world is pagan and idolatrous, then we have to be 'other.' But it is not necessarily a mitzvah just to be separate. It's a mitzvah to separate yourself from idolatry. It's a mitzvah to separate yourself from pagan brutality. It's a mitzvah to separate yourself from a culture that gives their children for Moloch worship. It's that you say no to. It's not just for the sake of being different."

Hartman lives in Jerusalem, where the ultra-Orthodox have become increasingly powerful and closed to the outside world. "Many people are rejecting secular knowledge, rejecting universities, because they feel that the very exposure to this type of larger world is going to eliminate the future of the Jewish people," he explained. "We have to fight against that type of 'return to the ghetto' mind-set as a necessary condition for Jewish survival."

Openness to the outside world is essential to making Judaism significant in North America today. It is also consistent with Judaism's history. One of the reasons Judaism has stayed alive for four thousand years is its ability to adapt to new circumstances and adopt new ideas, even while keeping the soul of its ethics, texts, and traditions. Jews have lived among many different peoples and cultures and borrowed from all of them. North African culture, Western European culture, Eastern European culture, Near Eastern culture, and North American culture, among many others, have all enriched Judaism.

Judaism as we know it in the United States and Canada was created by adaptation to the changing shape of North American life. The first large wave of Jewish immigrants, the German Jews of the mid–nineteenth century, sought acceptance among the Protestant ruling class, and in many ways the organizations they founded were modeled on those they encountered. They founded the men's club B'nai Brith when they were excluded from clubs like the Lions and Kiwanis; they built churchlike synagogues and developed religious practices that conformed to the shape of life in their new society. The large waves of Eastern European immigrants in the late nineteenth and early twentieth centuries lived and worked in the harsh conditions of tenements and factories, and their Yiddish culture was often inseparable from a fight for fair labor practices and living conditions.

During the rise of the counterculture in the 1960s and 1970s, a new embrace of ethnic identity led many Jews to reach back to their own roots and to explore spirituality and social activism through Judaism. Antiestablishment sentiment found its place in Jewish life as well, as young Jews rejected the institutions of their upbringing and rebuilt community according to new ideas, many of which have now become part of mainstream Judaism. The feminist movement inspired Jewish women to demand full inclusion in Jewish life and to reexamine what many considered outdated and sexist ideas and practices. While there is still a long way to go, women's participation in Jewish life—in communal leadership, in scholarship, in the rabbinate, in Jewish literature and culture—would not have been possible without an openness to ideas from the secular world and the courage to look beyond received truths.

How do we open Jewish life to ideas that are relevant for our moment in history? What do we have to do to assure a robust, significant Jewish future? I posed these questions to Rabbi Arthur Green, who for over thirty years has been a profound thinker and tireless innovator in Jewish life, as both a scholar and a communal leader. He is a professor emeritus at Brandeis University, the author of many books on Jewish mysticism and spirituality, and, most recently, rector of the transdenominational rabbinical school at Hebrew College in Boston. He is a founder of Havurat Shalom, which in 1968 inspired the creation of many other *havurot,* or small, informal groups that gather for creative forms of worship and community; and he has served as dean and president of the Reconstructionist Rabbinical College. What Green stands for resonates deeply with me, and I shall quote him extensively.

"We have to pass something down to the next generation that is richer because we had custody of it for a generation before," Green told me. "We have to have added something to it. If I were to give my kid exactly the same *Yiddishkeit* that my grandfather had in his shtetl in Lithuania, I'd be doing completely the wrong thing." His grandfather's Judaism, he said, "belonged to a world where there are two kinds of people, *yidn* and *goyim* [Jews and non-Jews], and they hated each other. That's all gone." His daughter needs "a very different kind of Jewish life." Green forcefully argued that we have to do more than preserve Judaism: "Some people think what you have to do is just keep it exactly as it was, without changing it, and pass it down. I call it Judaism in formaldehyde. There won't be anything alive in there."

How are today's young Jews different from those of his generation, who also sought to transform Jewish life? One difference, he explained, is their distance from the immigrant experience. At Brandeis, he said, "I was teaching kids who are fifth- and sixth-generation American Jews." As a grandson of immigrants himself, he grew up intimately familiar with "a sort of natural *Yiddishkeit*" that his grandparents brought to America: "These kids don't know what a Yiddish accent sounds like. They think gefilte fish was born in jars." While his own upbringing was rooted in Jewish neighborhoods and Jewish extended families, most of today's Jewish college students grow up in communities connected by factors other than kinship and ethnicity, and in almost half of the cases have only one Jewish parent. While they may feel some attachment to Judaism, they do not feel strongly rooted in Jewish life. They have not rejected Judaism and, as Green reflected, they were not as alienated by the Jewish education they received, as were their parents, who came of age in the 1960s and 1970s. But today's youth see Judaism as only one option in the array of choices in American society.

The sense of religion as choice is an integral part of

American life. Young Jews today are "really in the same seeking field as other Americans who know very little about their own traditions.... They could all choose anything." Green described the argument in a book called *The Heretical Imperative*, by the sociologist Peter L. Berger. Berger writes that the word "heresy" comes from the Greek word for choice.[5] In religious societies, Green explained, the very idea of choice contradicts the governing creed. In an open society, by contrast, choice defines your existence: "You can walk out into the crowd in New York and disappear, and nobody knows who you are, where you came from." Many of today's young Jews "are children of people who have already disappeared Jewishly." More than their parents, young Jews have a sense of floating in a world of options.

At the same time, Green said, many are interested in Judaism: "There is a hunger for Jewish learning in this generation that's much more widespread than it was in the *havurah* years."

I told Green that my goal is to get 100 percent of Jews to have some Jewish knowledge, because they can't be proud Jews if they don't know anything about Judaism. He concurred: "We'd like to give it to everybody. Not everybody will get it, of course. That's a dream. But if we push those percentage points up by ten or so, if we get into the double digits of increasing that knowledge, then we've done something tremendously worthwhile."

Today's Jews, he said, are better educated in general education, which makes the gap between their Jewish knowledge and their general knowledge more striking. Consider "the percentage of Jews we have with graduate degrees, who then get up in the synagogue and try to have an *aliyah* [reading from the Torah] and are illiterate." Knowledgeable Jews feel embarrassed about their ignorance in Jewish settings, and this sense of inadequacy drives them away. To feed the hunger for knowledge that exists among American Jews, we need education that doesn't talk down to people or make them feel like children. "Jewish life has a kind of a bad reputation, as being a place for unthinking, uncreative, conventional people," Green said. The North American Jewish community needs the kind of openness that will inspire talented, creative people to bring their energy into the sphere of Judaism.

Jewish Spirituality

What kind of ideas and Judaism will best suit today's Jews? Green began by asserting that he is "committed to a pluralistic vision" and that there is no "magic bullet that's going to solve all the problems of the Jewish people." There are many pathways to Jewish connection.

His own greatest involvement is in the area of Jewish religion and spirituality, particularly in "reintegrating the mystical tradition" into mainstream Judaism. While I have little connection to the world of Jewish mysticism or spiritual practices myself, Green's comments convinced me that a spiritually vibrant religious life is a crucial way to reach many of today's young Jews.

Green described the progress of his own thinking on

these matters from the 1960s and 1970s and the shape those ideas have taken today. He told me that when he graduated from the Conservative Movement's rabbinical school in 1967, he felt that there was not "a serious religious alternative to Orthodoxy for people who were real seekers." These were people "who took religious questions seriously, who wanted a personal and deep relationship to the tradition, who were becoming increasingly learned within the tradition, and yet who were not believers in the literal revelation of the Torah by God, or the absolute authority of the halacha." As he did himself, some of these seekers may have tried Orthodoxy but were not able to live with Orthodox attitudes toward non-Jews, toward non-Orthodox Jews, and, above all, toward women. The *havurah* movement came, in part, from this search for passion and intensity in Jewish practice and for a more intimate, informal setting for prayer as an alternative to the cathedral-like synagogues that had become standard in North America: "Why, I began to ask in 1970, did non-Orthodox Jews have to go to big synagogues of one thousand families, where you are known by the seat number of your ticket rather than by your name? Why couldn't there be a *shtiebel* [small communal prayer group] for non-Orthodox Jews?"

Over the past thirty years, he said, the synagogue has in many places changed and improved. Part of this is due to the *havurah* movement itself, whose influence led synagogues to adopt a more personal approach to building community, for example, by offering a variety of small prayer communities within one building. Change also came with distance from the immigrant experience. Now, he said, Jews are "comfortable enough with their own Americanness that they no longer need to prove it by a rabbi who speaks in golden tones and says 'thee' and 'thou' and that kind of thing that rabbis had to do in the 1950s." Synagogues have become more informal, and more and more have dialogues instead of sermons.

But the need for creativity and change in religious life is still there, Green continued. There are many Jews who have become serious religious seekers, and while some have turned to Orthodoxy, "a great many more have turned to Buddhism and other kinds of religious paths, or New Age cults of various kinds." Instead of dismissing all alternative religious paths as "cults," the Jewish community must examine why it fails to speak to those who are attracted to the Dalai Lama or to very serious religious teachers from the East. The Jewish mystical tradition has much to offer these seekers and should be made accessible to them.

Jewish religious life cannot afford to keep people out because they don't know enough: "These Indian teachers come West and they say, 'If you just close your eyes and breathe deeply and chant a few words, you are on the path.' When you go to a rabbi and you ask him to teach you the secrets of Kabbalah, he'll say, 'Do you keep kosher? Do you keep Shabbos? Do you know Hebrew?' And maybe ten years later we'll get to the good stuff; we'll get to the stuff you want."

At the same time, Green cautioned against watering Judaism down and making it superficial. He derided the now-popular version of "Kabbalah" popularized in the media as giving you some illusion of Kabbalah without any knowledge of Judaism. In contrast, he praised the Elat Chayyim retreat center in Connecticut, which offers Jewish meditation and chanting, and Congregation B'nai Jeshurun in New York City, where services are both spiritually uplifting and Jewishly grounded.

In his book *Ehyeh: A Kabbalah for Tomorrow*, Green offers religious seekers an accessible and inspiring explanation of Jewish mysticism and suggestions for what a Jewish spiritual practice might contain. Kabbalah is based in the mystical idea of the oneness of all reality.

> *[It] teaches that there is a secret unity of all Being, hidden within the multiplicity and diversity of life as we experience it.* God and universe are related not primarily as Creator and creature, *which sounds as though they are separate from one another, but as* deep structure and surface. *God lies within or behind the façade of all that is. In order to discover God—or the real meaning or the essential Oneness of Being—we need to turn inward, to look more deeply at ourselves and the world around us. Scratch the surface of reality and you will discover God.*

A practice of Kabbalah, as Green describes, involves an inner quest to understand yourself, and all of the world, as "an embodiment of divine light." This understanding inspires us to reshape our relationships, work, and daily life. Jewish ritual, prayer, and traditions are part of this reshaping, though the forms of observance will differ for each Jew. While some will find fulfillment in detailed observance of Jewish law, others may find their practice simpler but more deeply felt. "The important thing to remember is that, in acts of faith, quality rather than quantity counts," Green writes.

Green would like to create a Kabbalah that addresses the particular needs of our world today, a religious practice that makes us acutely aware of our responsibility to care for our earth and all its inhabitants. He writes:

> *Our suffering planet is deeply and urgently in need of healing. We humans stand in a moment when we must find teachings that will change our way of life, if we and our world are to go on living. A Kabbalah for tomorrow has to be seen as a Jewish contribution to a universal quest, a part of the reclaiming of the great spiritual traditions of humanity, a resource much neglected in the West for the past several hundred years.*[6]

A Jewish spiritual practice such as Rabbi Green describes can be a healing force that is both universal and deeply connected to our Jewish tradition.

Jewish Culture

For myself, prayer and spirituality are not the primary way I connect with Judaism. In my own Jewish practice, I prefer serious discussion of texts to song and prayer and find my strongest connection to Judaism through intellectual and ethical, not spiritual, pursuits. When I do pray, my personal goal is to find the inner strength to do what is right. When I speak to college students, I describe a practice I call the mirror test. Every day I look in the mirror upon arising and I ask myself if I like the person looking back at me. If I don't, I ask myself why not. Have I done something I should not have? Have I hurt another's feelings? Was I rude or overly aggressive? If so, I repent and try to make up for it with the person I injured.

In studying the Bible and Talmud, I find wonderful lessons on how to live one's life. The concept of not picking up the forgotten bits of the harvest but leaving them for the poor is a basic tenet of a very humanistic religion. Not doing to others that which is hateful to you is a basic way to live one's life. I first became interested in studying the Talmud because I find it to be a set of rules by which we could all live honorably with each other. I am proud that our sages wrote this wondrous epic so many years ago, while civilization was at its earliest stage of development.

Even as Jewish religious observance becomes more open to the kind of spiritual practice Arthur Green described, we must also be open to the idea that Judaism is a culture as well as a religion. The typical mind-set of Jewish leadership is still that to be an involved Jew you must join a synagogue and observe the laws governing Shabbat, kashrut, and the Jewish holidays. But there are many ways to connect with Judaism outside of ritual and prayer. Today, many Jews have embraced

Judaism through social activism, artistic expression, and intellectual study. We should look at Jewish texts and traditions as our shared culture and invite all to engage with them. Those who are more interested in traditions and ethics than in religious observance should also have their place in Jewish life, and it should not be at the margins. What Mordecai Kaplan, founder of the Reconstructionist Movement, wrote in 1934 still needs to be understood today: "Judaism . . . is something far more comprehensive than Jewish religion. It includes the nexus of a history, literature, language, social organization, folk sanctions, standards of conduct, social and spiritual ideals, esthetic values, which in their totality form a civilization."[7] Teaching Judaism as a rich culture and civilization that has adapted to many places and times, that has stayed open to the outside world even as it has maintained its own ethics, texts, and traditions, is essential to creating a significant Judaism for today.

Jewish education in this country has given too little attention to the texts, history, and culture of the Jewish people. In the supplementary schools (Sunday school and Hebrew school), children are too often mainly taught how to pray, and are prepared for the prayers they will need to become a bar or bat mitzvah. But after these rituals, and the parties and presents that accompany them, are completed, we lose many of our young people. This should be no surprise, if all that children have learned of Judaism is a series of rituals and words that seem disconnected from their lives. If we teach students that Judaism is a culture as well as a religion, we open up the wealth of Jewish life to those of many interests and beliefs, including those who consider themselves secular.

One of the foremost proponents of teaching Judaism as a culture is philanthropist Felix Posen. His Posen Foundation serves the needs of nonreligious Jews, who are referred to interchangeably as "secular" and "cultural." I prefer the term "cultural," as it implies a commitment to one's Jewish heritage, while "secular" may be understood simply as having an absence of belief. Among other projects, the Posen Foundation creates courses in cultural Judaism at universities, supports literary and bibliographic projects, and trains teachers. The list of subjects and authors that Posen hopes to cover in courses and publications is extensive, and gives an understanding of the depth of knowledge available, and also the depth of Posen's commitment.

Posen, who lives in London, grew up Orthodox in Brooklyn, New York. He remained *shomer Shabbat* (keeper of the Sabbath) until after university, when, as he described to me, "I came back to where I was brought up, and I just couldn't take it anymore. I gave up Orthodoxy. As I gave up the religion, I started looking into Judaism. For the first time I started understanding, very slowly."

Posen believes that nonreligious Jews can still be deeply engaged with the central texts of our tradition, including the Bible and the Talmud, which he sees as great pieces of literature: "The Bible could be taught as a literary novel, if you will, written by human beings and not by God."

While Posen's secularism goes beyond my own skepticism

about belief in God, I respect his tremendous efforts to seek full inclusion in Jewish life for self-defined secular or cultural Jews and to make Judaism's rich cultural and intellectual life available to all. Judaism has a great deal to offer even those who consider themselves secular. It emphasizes practice over belief. We are allowed to doubt even the existence of God and commanded to ask questions. Even a nonbeliever can find great value in weekly study of our Torah, which tells our founding stories and provides the basis of our ethics. It's fascinating to read what different scholars and rabbis have to say about each portion and to discuss their relevance for today. During different periods of Jewish history, Jews have debated whether it is study or prayer that should be at the center of Jewish life. Frequently, the *beit midrash,* or house of study, was more important to the Jewish community than the *beit tfilah,* or house of prayer. There is no reason that a Jewish practice with study at its center can't also be valid today.

The audience Posen hopes to reach in America is a large one: He told me that according to the 2001 American Jewish Identity Survey, conducted by the City University of New York Graduate Center and underwritten by the Posen Foundation, 40 percent of American Jews classified themselves as secular. He acknowledges, however, that most of these Jews know little about Judaism and that this is the group most likely to assimilate: "Most cultural Jews are Jewishly ignoramuses. They may be Nobel Prize winners, they may be brilliant scholars . . . but most of them don't know about their own culture." But unlike others who conclude from this idea that it isn't worth spending time and resources to reach this segment of the community, Posen believes that the problem is that Judaism is not properly taught as a culture. "We need to have programs for that sector of our people, everywhere in the world," he asserted.

Posen is active in promoting the teaching of Judaism as a culture in Israel, where the issues at stake are quite different than they are in North America. In the United States and Canada, our biggest problem is ignorance of even the basics of Jewish holidays and traditions. In Israel, where Hebrew is the language of daily life and Shabbat and the Jewish holidays make up the national calendar, all Israeli Jews possess a certain baseline of Jewish knowledge and many incorporate aspects of Jewish observance into their lives. But while North American Jews understand that there is a broad spectrum of religious practice, in Israel the state does not recognize Reform, Conservative, or Reconconstructionist Judaism and "religious" largely means Orthodox. Israeli Jews generally identify themselves with the categories of secular (hiloni), traditional (masorati), ultra-Orthodox (haredi), and Modern Orthodox (dati-leumi), and there is an antagonistic divide between the religious and secular sectors of the population.

This division between secular and Orthodox Israelis has its roots in the history of Zionism. During the eighteenth and nineteenth centuries, rabbis in Eastern Europe forbade Jews from immigrating to Palestine, saying the land of Israel may only come under Jewish control with the coming of the Messiah. For their part, the secular, socialist Zionists who founded the state repudiated religion angrily as a force blocking the Jews' path from oppression to liberation. While some early Zionists, influenced by the thinker known as Ahad Ha'am, called for a society based in renewed Jewish cultural life rather than political independence, a sense of Israeli nationalism was the more dominant force in the founding of the Jewish state. With the rejection of religion and the invention of the modern Israeli came a sense of disconnect from Jewish texts, culture, and peoplehood. While they are proud of their nation, many Israelis associate "Judaism," including study of our classical sources and ethics, with the ultra-Orthodox, whom they resent for their control of marriage, divorce, and funerals and for their exemption from army service. One might meet young Israeli Jews in the streets of Tel Aviv who, when asked whether or not they are Jewish, answer "We're Israelis." That is said with pride, as it should be, but why not have pride in being Jewish, too?

Secular Israelis should have a deeper understanding of what it means to be Jewish and a deeper sense of connection with their Jewish family around the world. Just as we need Jewish education for all Jews in the Diaspora, so the same thing is required in Israel's Jewish secular public schools, where there is little Jewish education beyond courses in the Bible and history that most agree are poorly taught. There is some progress, and, as recent survey data suggests, the lines in the sand between secular and religious may be becoming less stark.[8] But there is a long way to go. In the Jewish state, all Jews, whatever religious path they choose to follow, should be provided with a strong foundation in the texts, ethics, and history of Judaism.

Posen's projects in Israel speak to this need. One notable example is Alma Hebrew College in Tel Aviv. Alma is perhaps best know among Israelis for its wildly popular Tikkun Leil Shavuot (a night of study traditionally held on the holiday of Shavuot), during which thousands of secular Jews crowd into all-night lectures and study sessions on subjects ranging from the poetry of Natan Alterman to Talmudic texts. This event celebrates a religious holiday in a traditional way but does not imply that participants should take on Orthodox beliefs and practices. Instead, it gives them an opportunity to study, question, and celebrate their heritage in all its variety. In our conversation, Posen stressed that his aim is not to attack religion. "We look upon Judaism as a culture," he said. "And culture includes religion but is not only religion."

In both Israel and the Diaspora, secular Jews lack knowledge of the wealth of Jewish texts and traditions, and an important part of Posen's vision is to make this knowledge available. It is vital that we provide these many Jews with the means to discover that one can live a proud, involved Jewish life outside, or alongside, the life of the synagogue. We have to change our mind-sets and teach Judaism in a way that emphasizes culture as much as religious observance and belief. In our day schools and supplementary schools, in our programs for youth and for adults, we should teach the texts and traditions of our heritage in ways that inspire all, including the skeptics, the doubters, and the nonbelievers, to build an identity that is profoundly, pridefully, and authentically Jewish.

Chapter 4

RESPECT, NOT TOLERANCE: EMBRACING JEWISH DIVERSITY AND DIFFERENCE

North American Jews today are remarkably free from attacks from without. But within our own community, we are a fractured and a fractious people. Instead of letting our differences tear us apart from within, let's recognize, and celebrate, our diversity. North American Jewry is comprised of Jews with a great variety of religious beliefs, denominational affiliations, ethnic backgrounds, and family structures. Some call for tolerance, but I prefer the words "mutual respect." As an individual, I am not interested in being tolerated or in simply tolerating the presence of those who are different from me. We must build respect between the different segments of the Jewish community, through civil dialogue and debate. There should be room in the tent of Jewish peoplehood for all who choose to find shelter and community there, and an understanding that all voices should be respectfully heard: male and female, gay and heterosexual, from across denominational lines, and from all racial and ethnic backgrounds.

Religious Pluralism

One of the biggest problems in Judaism is the lack of respect among the different denominations. Our people simply do not know how to talk to each other and, more important, to listen. When Jews from different denominations debate, too often their goal is only to humiliate the others and destroy their points of view. We don't need to agree on everything, but more civility in the Jewish world would be very welcome by many who toil in those arenas. We have to understand our common need to cultivate an inclusive community, even as we define our differences. We will all be better off if we accept that religious pluralism is a sign of vitality that offers a variety of options to a Jewish population that most often is simply opting out of Judaism altogether.

Pluralism need not mean abandoning your own views. Avi Weiss, an Orthodox rabbi, told me that for him, pluralism means recognizing that while he and his Conservative and Reform colleagues may differ on crucial matters, they can "respectfully interact and dialogue." At the heart of a pluralistic vision is a sense of *ahavat Yisrael,* or love of the Jewish people. "I recognize that I have no monopoly on passionately loving the Jewish people or the land of Israel,"

Weiss said. "My Conservative and Reform colleagues have the same kind of love as I do. We have much to learn from each other. Our language about each other should never be negative."

As North American Jewry faces declining numbers of identified Jews, all denominations should share the goal of drawing more Jews to Judaism, whatever path the individual should choose to follow. Weiss told me that he would encourage a religious seeker to try a congregation to the left or the right of his own on the religious spectrum, if he thought that person would better find his or her path there. Too often, rabbis are trained to think about what is good for their ideological affiliation rather than what is good for Jewry. This attitude alienates young people, who don't understand the denominations and don't want to understand something that keeps Jews fighting among themselves.

Perhaps someday we won't call ourselves Orthodox, Reform, Conservative, or Reconstructionist Jews but simply Jews. The denominational divisions to which North American Jews are so accustomed are by no means the only way to think about Jewish practice. They are a modern phenomenon, which grew out of the attempt by European Jews, and then American Jewish immigrants, to integrate their religion into their identity as citizens of modern states. From the destruction of the Second Temple until modern times, the only formalized practice was traditional rabbinic Judaism, based on the study and observance of God's laws as written in the

Torah and expounded in the Talmud—both revered as given by God at Mount Sinai. The first important alternative sprang up in early-nineteenth-century Germany, when German Jews attempted to simplify the lengthy and repetitive Jewish prayers and to adapt Jewish law and ritual to liberal Western values and to the general culture. By the mid-nineteenth century, a Reform rabbinate arose in Germany. When German Jews came to North America during this period, they brought their "new" religion with them. The monument to their culture was Temple Emanu-El, on New York's Fifth Avenue, where for many years anyone who was so old-fashioned and out of step with this new Judaism that he dared wear a yarmulke was asked to remove it. Those who derided this attitude called Temple Emanu-El "the Cathedral" or "Our Lady of Fifth Avenue."

Rabbi Eric Yoffie, president of the Union for Reform Judaism, explained that the German Jews who established the Reform Movement in America "looked for a new kind of Judaism that would be appropriate to American soil and American culture." Their practice was a radical departure from traditional rabbinic Judaism, and in many ways sought to imitate the religious culture of America's Protestant ruling class. They deemphasized the idea of Jews as a culture and people, so that a Jewish "nationality" would not compete with their new identity as Americans. They emphasized God and ethics instead of ritual observance, and the complex laws of the Talmud were set aside in favor of the simpler laws of Moses laid out in the Bible. Today, Reform Judaism, while still emphasizing ethics and social justice, has become more traditional, with an increased focus on Jewish text study and prayer.

Those who, while not happy with the strictures of Orthodoxy, thought that Reform had gone too far created another stream of Judaism, which came to be known as the Conservative Movement. Conservative Judaism, which originated in mid–nineteenth century Germany as a response to the Reform Movement, held that it was important to "conserve" tradition, even while regarding Judaism as a living religion that could adapt to contemporary society. Conservative Judaism became a formal movement in America, and in 1902 Solomon Schechter transformed the Jewish Theological Seminary on New York's Upper West Side into the center of the new denomination.[1]

In the 1920s, Mordecai Kaplan, a Conservative rabbi and thinker, invented yet another stream of Judaism called Reconstructionism. I have been much affected in my own thinking by Kaplan. He regarded Judaism above all as a civilization, and his religious stream, which was formalized in 1968 with the creation of the Reconstructionist Rabbinic College, emphasized our history, texts, and traditions more than theology. The Reconstructionist prayer book has far more Hebrew than the Reform and a skeptical, questioning attitude toward belief in God and Jewish law that sets it apart from the Conservative Movement. The Reconstructionist Jews are a small but committed group.

The question may well be asked: Do these differing

streams enhance Judaism as a whole? They certainly did at one time. The denominations have been vital in helping North American Jews negotiate the balance between being American or Canadian and being Jewish and in keeping our tradition alive and relevant in the modern world. But increasingly, denominational identification is losing its significance. Religious belief and observance have become more individualized, as people seek personal fulfillment rather than affiliation with a broad movement. For many North American Jews today, the denomination to which they belong is less important than the character of the synagogue itself: its spiritual quality, music, or tradition of social activism. While the organized Jewish community continues to fight battles over the denominations, individual Jews are less concerned. More relevant to our changing community are those organizations whose visions encompass many viewpoints, and those new, independent communities that speak directly to the needs of particular groups. I will discuss many of these initiatives in the second part of this book.

The denominational platforms do offer clarity for those who seek to define their religious ideology, and it is a challenge to consider alternative models for Jewish religious practice. Rabbi Arthur Green, who, as mentioned, has founded a transdenominational rabbinical school, asked himself this important question: "If you're pluralistic does that mean that you don't have any ideology other than pluralism?" In answer to his own question, he reflected on the commitments he considers central to his own transdenominational Judaism: a commitment to studying the Jewish tradition, to learning the Hebrew language, and to *klal Yisrael*, a love of Jews that transcends boundaries. "Say what you stand for, not just what you're opposed to," he concluded. Let's also stand for mutual respect and hope that we can reach across our differences and learn from one another.

Inclusion of Women

In the Reform, Conservative, and Reconstructionist movements, women have achieved a remarkable degree of inclusion, especially when you consider that until 1972 there was no such thing as a woman rabbi. Rituals aimed at creating an egalitarian community, such as the bat mitzvah and baby naming for girls, have become widespread practice, and in the non-Orthodox movements women are included in a minyan (the group of ten required for prayer) and invited to read from the Torah. Still, there remain great strides to be made in increasing women's roles in religious and communal leadership across the denominations.

We spoke with Dr. Paula Hyman, professor of modern Jewish history at Yale University, about women's changing roles in the American Jewish community. The Jewish feminist movement, she said, took shape around 1970, as young women, primarily undergraduate and graduate students who were deeply involved in the Jewish world, "began to reflect on what it meant to be excluded from the mainstream of Jewish education, from the mainstream of religious leadership, from being counted in a minyan and having access to the Torah." Most of the progress, as she described it, happened on a grassroots level and reached an American population that was ready for an egalitarian Judaism. Now, about equal numbers of men and women are becoming rabbis, and many women have also entered the field of Judaic studies.

While she was optimistic about women's continued leadership and involvement in Jewish life, Hyman described a concern among women rabbis over the fact that so few women have become senior rabbis of large congregations. This may be due, in part, to the challenges of doing justice to this position while raising a family. Hyman suggested that instead of accepting the perceived definition of a rabbi or cantor, women can "develop new models for leadership" that enable both male and female congregational rabbis to find workable models for balancing career and family. Indeed, this idea was one of the main topics in our conversations with women rabbis. Rabbi Shira Milgrom is one of two senior rabbis at Congregation Kol Ami, a large Reform synagogue in White Plains, New York. She spoke about the synagogue's choice to form a "rabbinic partnership," in which two rabbis share the duties of head rabbi. For her, she said, this unusual choice "was very driven by what are considered traditional feminist models of the sharing of power as opposed to consolidating of power." Spiritual power, she said, must be shared, not hoarded. What's more, the partnership allows both rabbis to better integrate family and work, something "which is all the more challenging for Jewish professionals, because work time is often in direct conflict with Jewish family time." For a rabbi to "teach with integrity about being a Jewish parent, about having Shabbat at home," he or she must also live it.

We also spoke with Rabbi Angela Warnick Buchdahl, cantor at New York City's Central Synagogue. Buchdahl's own story is interesting: She was born in South Korea to a Buddhist, Korean mother and a "nominally affiliated" Reform Jewish father, and is the first Asian-American rabbi and cantor. She spoke generally about the challenge of being a woman and a committed Jew. As a female Jew, she said, you must constantly face the fact that Judaism's laws and traditions were created by men: "When you delve into the traditional texts, you have to search hard to find female voices. The challenge of being a female Jew is in part the struggle with the patriarchal nature of the tradition."

Buchdahl's comment underscores the point that cultivating an inclusive Judaism is about more than simply including women: We have to be aware of the biases and assumptions in our religion that have excluded so many generations of women's voices. In her book *Engendering Judaism*, Rachel Adler calls for both men and women to be aware of the role of gender in our tradition: "Relegating gender issues to women alone perpetuates a fallacy about the nature of Judaism. It presumes that Judaism is a body of gender-neutral texts and traditions, and that women constitute a special gendered addendum to the community of its transmitters."[2]

Among the Orthodox, men and women still have religious roles sharply defined by gender. Women have increasingly found greater equality, particularly in the area of study, and institutions such as Drisha, in New York, are helping to ensure that women are given the opportunity for the rigorous training that will enable them to take leadership roles. Still, in most Orthodox communities women's roles are restricted. Women cannot be counted in a minyan. In synagogues women and men are seated separately, and while in some Orthodox synagogues the room is divided equally between men and women, in others women are relegated to seats upstairs, in cramped and uncomfortable quarters. This reminds me of an argument between two rabbis, one Orthodox and one Conservative. The Orthodox rabbi insisted that women distract men from prayer and should be separated, preferably on a floor above and removed from the main sanctuary. The Conservative rabbi insisted that synagogue attendance was surely a family affair and that family members should pray together regardless of their gender. This argument went back and forth with variations on the same theme. Finally, the Conservative rabbi looked at his colleague and said, "Perhaps you're right. In your synagogue, if men and women sat together, during the sermon they would surely sleep together."

Orthodox laws surrounding marriage and divorce keep

women dependent on their husbands' wills and in my view are terribly unjust. In Israel, they affect not only the Orthodox community but all Israeli Jews, since the state-appointed Orthodox rabbinate controls the marriages, divorces, and funerals of all Jews. To effect a marriage, the groom gives the bride a ring before two male witnesses. To divorce, according to Biblical law, the husband "writes [the wife] a bill of divorcement, hands it to her, and sends her away from his house."[3] A woman has no power to end a marriage herself. This Biblical law and the Talmudic laws derived from it give a man the power to keep his wife trapped in an abusive or neglectful marriage. It has also opened the door to abuses by men who force their wives to relinquish property in exchange for a get, a bill of divorcement. A woman whose husband refuses her a get or who is missing, and thus unable to grant one, is called an *agunah*, or chained woman, as she cannot remarry.

Within the Orthodox community, both in North America and in Israel, there are courageous and innovative leaders who are working within the framework of halacha to challenge and change these laws and to deepen and expand the role of women in ritual, learning, and communal life. In Jerusalem, I spoke with Dr. Tova Hartman, who is as brilliant as she is passionate about her synagogue, Kehilat Shira Chadasha (which means "community of new song"). The synagogue is Orthodox, but it requires two minyanim, ten women as well as ten men. It is this innovation that has attracted attention to Shira Chadasha, but for Hartman the principle of inclusion goes deeper. All of the shul's activities, she said, are based around the principle of *chesed,* or kindness: For example, at each service a greeter on the men's side and the women's side welcomes each individual and takes the elderly or those who need help to their seats, and each week a different family is responsible for hosting Shabbat dinner for those who have nowhere to go. "Feminism teaches all about the invisibility of women," Hartman said. "I want to take that principle of invisibility and bring it to the invisibility of people in general." How, she asks, "do we create a religious place where nobody is invisible, where your being counts; where you know that if you're not there, somebody notices; that if you need something, somebody notices?" Nine synagogues modeled on Shira Chadasha have opened in the United States, she told me, and she has cautioned them, "Do not copy just the egalitarianism. Our feminism means something deeper than only just the fact that women are leading parts of prayer services, or that they have Aliyot, or that they *leyn* [read Torah]. Our feminism is about bringing the traditional women's roles of hosting and taking care of people . . . to the center stage of a shul's life."

Inclusion of Gay and Lesbian Jews

Gay and lesbian Jews have increasingly made inroads into the Jewish community, but we have a long way to go toward making Jewish life a place where these Jews are afforded the respect they deserve. There has been some progress among the movements in recent years. The Reform and Recon-structionist movements will both ordain openly gay rabbis and bless gay commitment ceremonies and marriages (though within the Reform Movement there has been controversy over whether or not gay marriages fit into the legal category of *kiddushin,* or holiness, which defines marriage). In 2007, the Conservative Movement also voted to admit students who are openly gay into its rabbinical schools and to permit its rabbis to bless gay commitment ceremonies. However, the ruling specifies: "It is not possible to set aside the explicit Biblical prohibition on anal sex that is stated twice in Lev-iticus and frequently reaffirmed by the rabbis."[4] In other words, a gay man can become a rabbi only if he makes the commitment to refrain from anal sex (lesbians are unaf-fected by this). While this decision is celebrated by many activists, gay and heterosexual, who have led the struggle in the Conservative Movement, other gay rights proponents find it invasive and reflecting a general attitude of ambi-valence and disrespect toward gay and lesbian Jews. In the Orthodox world, gay and lesbian Jews face wrenching ques-tions, though there has been some progress in raising aware-ness and building support. Sadly, on the whole gay and lesbian Jews still find prejudice and exclusion across the Jewish com-munity.

Religious opposition to homosexuality is based on the statement in Leviticus that is translated: "Do not lie with a male as one lies with a woman; it is an abhorrence."[5] There has been much debate and discussion concerning the origins of this statement, ranging from a perception that homosexuality was associated with idolatry, to a belief that sexual activity between males was demeaning to males (relegating them to the status of women), to the belief that it was problematic because it didn't lead to procreation. However, the key point seems to me that as with many laws in the Torah, the prohibitions against homosexuality were created in the context of conditions that are no longer relevant to our community today. Our community is only now beginning to recognize that gays and lesbians are God's children, too, with equal rights, equal aspirations, and equal contributions to the commonweal. They should be entitled to marry, to raise families, and to partake in all the joys and responsibilities that come with being a committed Jew.

We spoke with Rabbi Sharon Kleinbaum, who leads Congregation Beth Simchat Torah (CBST), in New York City's West Village, the largest gay and lesbian synagogue in the country. When CBST was founded in 1973, Kleinbaum said, "not a single Jewish organization . . . national or local, openly welcomed openly gay people." While "of course we know there were always gay people in Jewish life," to be actively involved in the Jewish community "you had to look straight, even if you weren't straight." As an openly gay Jew, "there was absolutely no way of being active, either as a layperson or as a rabbi, in the Jewish community—until 1973 and the formation of CBST and, three months earlier, the formation of the gay synagogue in Los Angeles."

Today, Kleinbaum said, there are many synagogues where

gay and lesbian Jews are welcome. Yet there is a still a sense in the "dominant Jewish community" that "everybody has to be heterosexual" and the rabbi must "have *x* number of kids" and look exactly like the people in his or her community. Kleinbaum's own commitment is to "understanding that Torah is going to be learned not just from people who look exactly like us, but from people who are going to challenge us to think differently." The fact that CBST, a gay and lesbian synagogue, has a heterosexual associate rabbi, Ayelet Cohen, reflects this commitment to diversity and challenge.

Kleinbaum's comments on the synagogue's membership also reflect her celebration of diversity: "We're economically extremely heterogeneous, because we're not just based in neighborhoods.... At CBST we have people who are virtually homeless, literally living in shelters, and people who are living in multimillion-dollar town houses in the West Village." The synagogue also attracts nongay members, mostly young people who "are also rejecting these rigid borders between gay and straight" and who want to be part of an inclusive community.

All synagogues should become fully inclusive of gay and lesbian Jews. They may find their congregants more receptive than they anticipate. Rabbi Harold Schulweis told me that when he decided to actively welcome gay and lesbian Jews in his Conservative synagogue in Los Angeles he was at first hesitant. His wife told him, "You're going to lose a lot of people. But if you think it's in your bones, do it."

The response to his sermon, which he delivered on Rosh Hashanah, was overwhelmingly positive: "I never in my fifty years [as a rabbi] got a standing ovation, as I did after that sermon." He realized that almost everyone in the congregation has someone in his or her family who is gay. What's more, Schulweis told me, the gay and lesbian Jews he began to work with were a remarkably committed group. At first their choice to be part of the Conservative Movement surprised him. He would say, "Listen, why don't you go to Reform?" But they wanted a more traditional synagogue and were willing to persevere even in a movement that at the time did not recognize homosexual rabbis or bless gay commitment ceremonies. Gay and lesbian Jews, who have had to struggle with so much hostility in North American Jewish life, have much to contribute, and their voices must be heard.

Racial and Ethnic Diversity

What does the "typical" Jewish family look like? Many picture two Ashkenazic Jews and their two biological children. But this image does not reflect the reality of the North American Jewish population today. The Jews, who have lived among people all over the world, have always been racially diverse. This diversity exists in the North American Jewish community, and it should be recognized and celebrated.

Dr. Gary A. Tobin, president of the Institute for Jewish &

Community Research in San Francisco, conducted a study (together with Diane Tobin and Scott Rubin) of racial and ethnic diversity in the American Jewish community. Tobin found that of the 6 million Jews he counts in the United States, there are roughly 1.2 million, or 20 percent, who are African-American, Asian-American, Latino, Sephardic (Spanish and Portuguese), Mizrahi (of Middle Eastern descent), and mixed-race. This includes Latinos whose families were forced to convert during the Spanish Inquisition, African-American Jewish communities, and many multiethnic spouses, children, and relatives of Jews who are closely connected with the Jewish community and practice many Jewish customs.[6] Tobin cited racially diverse leaders in America, including Rabbi Capers Funnye, leader of the Beth Shalom B'nai Zaken Ethiopian Hebrew Congregation, an African-American synagogue in Chicago, and Rabbi Rigoberto Emmanuel Viñas, rabbi of Lincoln Park Jewish Center in Yonkers, a first-generation Cuban-American who discovered that his family was descended from *anusim*, the Hebrew term for Jews who were forced to convert during the Spanish Inquisition: Rabbi Viñas is the founder and director of El Centro de Estudios Judíos "Torat Emet," a Spanish-language Jewish education and spirituality center for Jews from all over Latin America. Tobin also described an annual Chanukah party attended by over four hundred Jews of diverse backgrounds, including European, African, Asian, and Latino, and other events and programs organized for diverse Jews in San Francisco.

Tobin praised the commitment and contributions of those he interviewed and surveyed for his study. Jews who defy the model of the "typical" American Jew often have to work harder to find their place in Jewish life and are forced to confront the attitude that they are not "real" Jews. Despite a Jewish community that often doesn't give them much help, many have chosen to play active roles in Jewish life. "They are passionate about it and bring vibrancy to the Jewish people," Tobin asserted.

Rabbi Angela Warnick Buchdahl spoke about her own experience of the Jewish community's limited vision. As a rabbi she is a Jewish "insider," she said, but for most of her life she has had the status of outsider in the Jewish community: "It's in part because I have a non-Jewish mother; it's in part because I look Asian and not just Jewish. . . . I don't think it was a particularly friendly place for me, frankly. I had lots of questioning about if I was really a Jew." Buchdahl challenged the American Jewish community to understand the real picture of American Jewish life today. She pointed out that many Jewish couples have adopted children from other cultures and there are many Jews not only in interfaith marriages but in interracial marriages as well. This multiracial character is "the new face of Judaism," which, she pointed out, is in some ways "as old as the Bible."

In Buchdahl's view, the American Jewish community also needs to rethink its "Ashkenazic assumption" about Jewish culture, from the foods that are considered Jewish to the Eastern European sound of the traditional *chazanut* (cantorial music). Ashkenazic Jewish culture represents just one "specific region of Jewish history," she said, yet it is considered as "Jewish with a capital J." By "recognizing, celebrating, and reacquainting ourselves with the diversity of the Jewish historic experience" we will better reflect the reality of the Jewish community. Jewish culture has always been enriched by other cultures. Today, "we not only lose people because we make them feel less welcome, but we're losing an opportunity for enriching our own Jewish community."

Fostering a Jewish community that is open, welcoming, and diverse is more than a practical measure to ensure Judaism's survival as our numbers shrink in North America. To cultivate these qualities in our community is to offer an important alternative to the worldwide religious zealotry that in recent years has been the source of so much violence and hatred. Perhaps the most dangerous word in the English language is "believe." Countless millions have been slain in wars caused by religious rivalry, by the attitude "I have the certain truth, and if you don't accept it, I will kill you." Zealotry is not confined to any one religion. While Muslim zealotry is on everybody's mind, other religions have their own zealots. In Israel, there are Jewish zealots who believe that in order to bring the Messiah, the entire Biblical land of Israel must be under Jewish control. One of these fanatics murdered Yitzhak Rabin.

My father, of blessed memory, taught his children to be

moderate in all things. Being a rather cheeky son, I once challenged him, saying, "But Father, to be perfectly consistent, you must also be moderate in your moderation." I then ducked, knowing the well-deserved kick in the pants was coming. I now realize just how important moderation has become. The Jewish religion, while it has always had strains of zealotry and fanaticism, has an even stronger tradition of openness and questioning. Engaging multiple viewpoints is one of the hallmarks of Judaism, as expressed in the old saying "two Jews, three opinions." To become a proud Jew should not mean finding a certain truth that blinds you to all other viewpoints. The Talmud is full of differing points of view. When it resolves an issue in favor of one opinion, it doesn't expunge those that weren't adopted but leaves them there to acknowledge differences. One passage in the Talmud relates that after years of divisive disagreement between the schools of the sages Hillel and Shammai a *bat kol* (literally the "daughter of a voice," meaning a small voice from God) calls out, "Both these and these are the words of the living God."[7] Even as the voice resolves in favor of Hillel, it teaches that differing positions are valid and, more than that, vital.

The Jewish community should not be a fortress in which we protect and defend our beliefs but an open tent in which we challenge and discuss them. In this tent, we should find questions, not answers. We should find the ethical base that enables us to live in peace and justice with our fellow human beings, not the religious dogma that leads us to war with them. As Ruth's acts of kindness in the Bible bring her across boundaries and, ultimately, the story goes, make redemption possible, with a spirit of openness we can begin to heal our fractured people and bring a healing force to our fractured world.

Part II

———❧❧———

MAKING
RENAISSANCE
HAPPEN

Chapter 5

"GO AND LEARN":
OUR PLAN OF ACTION

How, in practical terms, do we foster a renaissance in Jewish life? The great sage Hillel was once asked by a potential convert to describe the entire Torah while standing on one foot. Hillel's response was, "That which is hateful to you do not do to your fellow. That is the whole Torah; the rest is explanation; go and learn."[1] I see in this story a kind of guide for how to approach a transformation of Jewish life. In the first sentence, Hillel expresses the profoundly humanistic imperative at the heart of Judaism. All of our work in Jewish life should be governed by this rule. As we re-examine our community and begin new initiatives, we must constantly ask whether we help to uphold the ethical commitment that is Judaism's great gift to civilization. Does our Jewish practice help improve our behavior toward our families? Our communities? The world?

Then, Hillel tells us to "go and learn." He does not offer a lecture about what to learn; he simply provides the imperative to discover Judaism for yourself. The best efforts to foster Jewish renaissance do not dictate what it means to be a good Jew but instead open up many pathways into the Jewish tradition. For some, this will be an intellectual path; for others, a spiritual one. Some will find their Judaism through traditional ritual observance, others through music, or study, or political activism. But the key is to keep learning. We must never see an end to our own Jewish education and never close our ears to voices new and old that challenge our own Jewish choices and practices.

In building a community united by ethics and learning, we offer a meaningful answer to the question of how to keep our culture alive in an open society. Most of the Jewish immigrants who arrived in the late nineteenth and early twentieth centuries knew relatively little about Judaism themselves but assumed their children would always be Jewish, just as in the Old Country they'd always been Jewish. The society in which they lived had never allowed them to be anything else. It never occurred to them, or perhaps even to their children, what a welcoming and wide-open society they would eventually find in North America. For generations, Jews did their best to blend into the melting pot, until we realized that we could disappear into it altogether. Hassidic Jews have one kind of answer to this danger: They preserve their Judaism by keeping themselves separate, with strict observance and with costumes of the Eastern European shtetl. This kind of Judaism has little to offer to the world at large. I would like North American Jews to be proudly Jewish in a way that helps to improve the world, rather than one that devotes its energy to keeping the world out.

The imperative "go and learn" is a call for action, not retreat. Instead of asking how we can preserve and protect what we have, we must empower our youth to reach into our tradition and discover a force for positive change. The Jewish tradition is full of wisdom on questions of how we treat our fellow human beings and our world. Judaism celebrates life and for centuries has sought ways to enrich it in joyous festivals and rituals and to examine and improve it through rigorous ethical inquiry. The answers our tradition provides are never simple, but they give us ways to grapple with the thorny questions that have become especially urgent as we confront a world rife with violence, poverty, and environmental destruction. If Jewish youth can be inspired to go and learn about Judaism, they will find ways to celebrate and better their lives and the lives of many others, within and beyond the Jewish community.

Those of us who care about the future of Judaism must get behind efforts to make this possible. We must invest time, money, and energy in Jewish education. We must set aside our differences and open lines of communication across the Jewish community—between religious and secular, between large established institutions and small grassroots initiatives, between old and young. We must also take a hard look at what we are doing and ask where energy and resources need to be redirected. Are we holding on to institutions and attitudes that are left over from a different era, when our greatest need was to protect ourselves and build better lives? Are we focusing on preventing intermarriage at the expense of encouraging education? Do our synagogues, schools, youth groups, and camps teach a Judaism that will inspire our youth to make it their own?

Today's Jewish youth are uniquely positioned to create a joyful, ethical, and educated community. Jews of my generation grew up with fear of the Nazis and with the experience of anti-Semitism in North American society. While we may feel strongly connected to our Jewish community, we have also struggled with the sense that to be regarded as fully American or Canadian one must seem less Jewish. We have always known we were Jewish but too often didn't know what made us Jewish, outside of the fact that we were born to Jewish parents. We grew up in strongly identified Jewish families and married Jews, but many of us have not adequately communicated to our children why Judaism matters, to us or to the world. Today's Jewish youth define their identity as Jews themselves—it is not imposed on them by "the others." In this multicultural society, they do not regard asserting themselves as Jews as counter to their identity as citizens of the United States and Canada. They are comfortable in their society and do not look over their shoulders to see who might attack them. Well educated and well off, they are not concerned with bettering themselves in the eyes of others but with finding ways to bring meaning into their own lives.

Today's Jewish youth, in short, look to Judaism with hope, not fear, and it is a Judaism of hope that we must foster. Instead of trying to pass on the Jewish life created by their parents, grandparents, and great-grandparents, let's give Jewish youth the opportunity to make Jewish life anew. Let's provide them with the opportunity to study the texts of our tradition but not tell them how they must interpret them. Let's help them to encounter the State of Israel but allow them to decide for themselves how they will view its actions and its role in their own lives. Let's encourage our Jewish youth to explore their religious practice and spiritual lives, without telling them what they must believe or pushing them into outdated denominational categories. Let's consolidate institutions that have lost their relevance, particularly the multiple organizations that still focus on fighting anti-Semitism. Let's open our ears to those who would challenge received wisdom and let go of the fear that tries to close down conversation. To keep the flame of Judaism alive, let's pass the torch to our children, so that they may lead Judaism to a new, brighter future.

There is much exciting work under way, and I will not attempt to describe all of it here. What I would like to share is my experience with particular initiatives that are making change happen. These initiatives fall into three broadly defined approaches, which I use to organize the chapters that follow:

I. BRING JEWISH LIFE TO LARGE NUMBERS OF JEWISH YOUTH. If they are to take up the torch of Jewish life, young Jews need a meaningful encounter with Judaism: its texts, traditions, and community. While there is new energy and excitement in Jewish life, it still touches only a fraction of Jews. Broad-based initiatives aim to bring Judaism to all North American Jewish youth.

2. PASS THE TORCH TO A NEW GENERATION OF LEADERS. Individuals make change happen. Among our Jewish youth are those who will lead in any field they choose. To bring their energy and creativity to Jewish life, we need to bring them into conversation with the Jewish tradition and with each other.

3. UPDATE OUR INSTITUTIONS. Throughout the twentieth century, the North American Jewish community developed remarkably effective institutions to meet the needs of that time. Today's Jewish youth, however, largely keep their distance from these institutions. We need to redirect our resources and infrastructure toward projects that are relevant to young Jews.

The initiatives I will write about differ in many ways, but they share qualities that are at the heart of their success and at the heart of a renaissance in Jewish life. They engage instead of preach, inspiring young people to learn more, rather than telling them exactly what they must believe. These initiatives convey that Judaism is a culture as well as a religion and that there are pathways to Jewish involvement outside of ritual and prayer. They help young Jews to appreciate the joy in Judaism and to cultivate a deeply Jewish sense of responsibility for our fellow human beings and for our world.

They create diverse, pluralistic environments and encourage mutual respect among Jews of differing perspectives. At the root of all of the programs is a sense of Jewish pride and of shared peoplehood that, despite our differences, must hold us together as Jews.

Chapter 6

HILLEL, BIRTHRIGHT ISRAEL, AND JEWISH CAMPING: BRINGING JEWISH LIFE TO LARGE NUMBERS OF JEWISH YOUTH

A Jewish renaissance is under way. Innovation is flourishing, as young Jews embrace Jewish culture and find new models for ritual and community. But the number of Jews who can attest to the vibrancy in Jewish life is still small. We need to think big and hold on to the hope that all North American Jews may be inspired to learn about their tradition.

This chapter will discuss several efforts to reach out to the majority of Jews in North America and beyond. These efforts do not advance a particular movement or mode of observance; instead, they get young people excited about Judaism so that they may seek out their own paths. In my conversations with those who lead and participate in these initiatives, I have found that this excitement is contagious. If we offer programs such as Hillel, Birthright Israel, and Jewish camping the support they need, we can imagine a Jewish life in which young people are inspired to create a new kind of Judaism, one that is infused with joy and pride, that opens its doors to welcome all, and that reaches out to make the world a better place.

Hillel International: Opening the Door to Jewish Life

Hillel: The Foundation of Jewish Campus Life has in recent years become an important engine for Jewish renaissance. Hillel is uniquely positioned to reach large numbers of Jews in North America. The vast majority (an estimated 85 percent) of North American Jews attend college. In college, students are free to make choices about how they will spend their time—they choose their own classes, activities, and friends. They are also at a crucial period of self-exploration and experimentation, which lessens as they graduate and enter the workforce. Hillel at its best is a place where Jewish college students explore Jewish culture and learning, where they become part of a pluralistic Jewish community, where they are active as Jews even as they explore their other interests in the diverse college environment.

As an organization, Hillel has had a complex journey to Jewish renaissance. Hillel thrived through the 1950s as a "home away from home" for Jewish students in college environments that were often hostile to Jews, primarily by offering kosher food and a place to pray. But through the next decades, Hillel faded in significance. By the late 1980s, most Jewish students wouldn't come near Hillel, and most Jewish professionals saw Hillel as an undesirable place to work.

Starting in 1988, under the charismatic leadership of Richard Joel, Hillel has updated itself to reach into the lives of young Jews today. A brief look at the nature of this transformation demonstrates the qualities at the heart of Hillel's change, qualities that are vital if we are to reach our youth and inspire a renaissance in Jewish life. While the earlier incarnation of Hillel provided a place for prayer and kosher food, the reinvented Hillel has at its heart an emphasis on Jewish learning, social action, and culture, along with offering services for Shabbat and Jewish holidays. Many of today's Jewish youth do not consider themselves religiously observant but are drawn to other aspects of Jewish life. Hillel chapters are pluralistic, inviting all who wish to identify themselves as Jews to participate and to lead. Jewish youth do not for the most part identify with the large denominational divisions, and diversity of belief and opinion inspires dynamism and debate. Hillel is part of the fabric of campus life, and being involved in Hillel does not mean turning your back on the experience of the diverse campus environment. The hope is that by the time students graduate from college, this experience will have given them a model for being Jewish in a way that is fully engaged with the world.

I became involved in Hillel in 1994, when the organization was in the throes of separation from its parent organization, B'nai Brith. B'nai Brith, which was once the largest and most significant Jewish communal organization, had adopted Hillel in 1925, two years after it was founded at the University of Illinois. When Richard Joel became international director, part of his task was to guide Hillel toward independence from B'nai Brith, which could no longer afford the $4 million that made up a quarter of Hillel's annual budget. As part of this transition, Joel was seeking support from philanthropists.

I will speak about Joel a great deal, because he has been such an influential force in Jewish renaissance and in my own understanding of it. From our early meetings, I was drawn to him and to his vision for change at Hillel. In his words and his demeanor, he conveyed a deep love of the Jewish people. He was clearly so secure in his Jewishness, with a black and white yarmulke on his mostly black hair. He was extraordinarily intelligent. He was dedicated and conveyed a great faith in the idea that Hillel would change things. He inspired trust and convinced me to join him at Hillel, where I became chairman of the Board of Governors.

One vital change at Hillel has been to introduce the term "Jewish renaissance." The previous community buzzword, "Jewish continuity," failed to inspire young people to become involved in Jewish life. The fear for Jewish survival, so deep in me and in my generation, is not a motivating force for them. Judaism has to be presented as something living and dynamic, something they can make their own, not as a relic they are obliged to reverently preserve and pass on.

The language of renaissance has vigor and challenges Jewish youth to create Jewish life anew. It is also more than public relations. You can't just tell Jewish youth that the future is theirs. You must trust in them and empower them to lead. You must act on your convictions, and Joel did this with amazing effectiveness as he changed Hillel from an outdated institution to a force for Jewish renaissance.

Joel recognized that most students saw their campus Hillel house as a place dominated by a small group of religiously observant Jews and that this had to change. Hillel can no longer play the role of "synagogue on campus," with a focus on Shabbat, kashrut, and holiday services. Many of the students he spoke with believed that becoming active as a Jew could only mean becoming religiously observant. While they had not rejected Judaism, they did not consider themselves religious and felt that they didn't belong at Hillel. Joel realized that he "didn't view Judaism as a religion; it was my civilization, my culture, the sea in which I swam." It was then, he told me, that he "stopped talking about Judaism and started talking about Jewishness." He wanted students to see "Jewishness" as something that encompasses Jewish ethics, Jewish literature, music, and film, Jewish history and traditions, something that belongs as much to them as it does to those who go to synagogue every week.

Richard identified two kinds of Jewish students on campus. One group, the minority, have come to college knowing "that they really want to be involved in their Jewishness." These are "empowerment students," and Hillel's job is to give them opportunities for leadership and action. The second group, the "silent majority," are "engagement students." The goal with these students is to help them "to take ownership of the Jewish story." The same categories offer a useful way to regard not only Jewish college students but all of North American Jewry. Those who are committed to their Judaism need to be given support, resources, and opportunities for leadership. Those who are disconnected from Jewish life—the majority of North American Jews—need first to be inspired.

To reach the "silent majority," Joel emphasized another point that all who seek to foster Jewish renaissance should note: that Hillel must reach students "where they are." Literally, this means bringing Jewish life to residence halls and fraternities and sororities. It also means showing students the Jewish relevance in their existing interests and activities, learning about the Jewish ideas of *tzedek,* meaning "justice," and *tikkun olam,* repair of the world, as they engage in community service work, or exploring Jewish music, art, and film. Through Hillel, students now work in soup kitchens, organize photography exhibitions, debate Talmudic texts and contemporary Jewish literature, and "do Jewish," as Joel called it, in a host of other ways. A practice of Judaism, all should recognize, need not isolate us. Indeed, Jewish practice should reach out and transform the world.

Before he left Hillel in 2002, Joel and I visited over

ninety campuses together, flying around the country in the private jet Joel liked to call "Hillel One." The aim of these visits was to get a sense of what was happening at the local level, to build support for Hillels in their home communities, and to meet students. These visits continued with Avraham Infeld, Joel's successor, and subsequently with Wayne Firestone, Hillel's current president. I always find them energizing. More than talking to the students, I enjoy listening to them. We tell students to be absolutely frank, not to just say what they think we want to hear. They usually comply and speak their minds. Hearing what students are thinking and talking about keeps me young, and it helps me to understand the real issues that we in the Jewish community face. I have had many conversations about intermarriage, which has helped me to see that we will only lose young people if we try to tell them whom they should or should not marry. While community leaders intone about the dangers of intermarriage, students, even those who are dedicated to Judaism, usually say that they can't guarantee they won't fall in love with a non-Jew. Young people do not want their elders telling them what to do. But if they are treated with honesty, respect, and intelligence, they are very receptive to learning more about their culture and heritage and only need some support to engage further.

There are great differences among the quality of Hillel chapters, and the major factor is the degree to which students run the show. The better the director, the more one sees of students. I remember in particular one visit to North-western University, just outside of Chicago. At lunch students introduced a film, and at the Hillel house afterward the director didn't show his face except to introduce one student at the beginning of the presentation. From then on, the students did everything. Joel was very proud of this, as it confirmed his style of management: make the students feel empowered and let Hillel houses belong to them. It is their leadership that is vital for our Jewish future.

Joel and I also instituted an hour of text study into our agenda on all of our visits. Jewish renaissance is grounded in Jewish learning: Hillel wants students to learn something at every event and has incorporated Jewish text study, long the standby of the yeshiva, into many of its activities. Central to the tradition of text study is the age-old method known as *hevruta*, which comes from the Hebrew word for "friendship." Two students sit together with a text between them and talk out loud about what they think it means. One thought leads to another, and if you have two good students, each gets double value from the session. As we invite students to read and debate the texts of our tradition, we invite them to take ownership of the Jewish story—to add their voices to centuries-old debates and make our texts relevant for today.

These text study sessions are tremendously enjoyable as well as educational. I remember sitting with a student at the Harvard Hillel, discussing why Aaron took on such a central role in the idolatry of the Israelites by building the Golden Calf while waiting for Moses to descend from the top of Mount Sinai. We discussed what must have been going through Aaron's head, for we knew he could not be an idolater. We concluded that he saw his job as keeping order and avoiding an open revolt while awaiting his brother. The Israelites were insecure about the invisible God that had taken them out of the land of Egypt, feeling so especially with the absence of Moses, and wanted a more tangible god like those the Egyptians had worshipped. We agreed that the moral lesson was prioritization: Refusing to build the idol would have resulted in chaos, and keeping order until the return of Moses was therefore the right thing to do. In fact, Aaron is known by the tradition as a lover of peace. In looking back into our ancient story, we were able to hone in on ethical questions that are still fresh and, in the process, build a dynamic community of learning.

At Hillel, this community has expanded to Jews around the world. All Jews are a single family, and a key part of Jewish renaissance is building a sense of peoplehood that crosses national boundaries. In doing so, we discover the diversity of culture and experience that keeps our tradition dynamic even as we discover the strengths that hold us together. The challenges that North American Jewry faces today are not unique but take different forms across the world.

There are currently Hillels in Latin America, the former Soviet Union, and Israel. Latin American Jewry faces the same issues that we do in North America: assimilation and a diminishing Jewish population. Unlike North American students, almost all students in Latin America live at home and commute to the classroom. Thus, Hillel houses that bring

Jewish students together to meet and, in some cases, to live can make a profound impact. Hillels opened in Argentina, Uruguay, and Brazil and have received enthusiastic receptions. I was fascinated to learn that in Montevideo, Uruguay, over 75 percent of the eligible Jewish college students had signed up! At the opening of a Hillel house in Buenos Aires, the excitement was palpable, despite the grip of the economic recession.

In the former Soviet Union, strengthening Jewish identity among college students poses a different challenge. Because of the repression of religion under Communism, most Russian Jews grew up with little experience with Jewish learning or practice. While North American college students may associate Jewish education with negative experiences at synagogues and Hebrew schools, Russian students often enter the university with their Jewish identity as a blank slate. They are hungry for knowledge and receptive to efforts to build Jewish community.

Lynn Schusterman and her late husband, Charles, were the basic movers in establishing the twenty-seven Hillel chapters that now exist in the former Soviet Union. The American Joint Distribution Committee, which works with Jews in need worldwide, was her partner in this endeavor. Schusterman is attempting, with some success, to motivate local Jews to become involved in supporting the Hillel chapters in their communities.

She described for me how these Hillels work. In big cities, where colleges do not have campuses and Hillel houses, students meet in apartments where they "create their own little Hillels." They have formed many clubs, focused on English, Hebrew, computers, business, Jewish learning, and even Yiddish. Schusterman went on to say, "I think what is so interesting about some of these kids is that they really did not know that they were Jewish. The only way they knew was that on their identity papers it said they were. They were not raised in Jewish homes. For them, being Jewish is a very special gift, and they hungrily embrace Judaism. There are Torah classes, and they want to learn everything they possibly can about it."

People sometimes ask why we have Hillels in Israel. Why would we need to build Jewish identity in the Jewish state? One of the troubling things about this generation of Israelis is that they are simply not Jewish enough. The religious-secular split in Israel has served to turn many people away from their heritage. Hillel in Israel seeks to inspire Israeli Jewish students from many backgrounds to take ownership of their Judaism. Chapters have been established at most of the major universities in Israel and at several colleges, including Hebrew University in Jerusalem, Tel Aviv University, Haifa University/Technion, the Interdisciplinary Center Herzliya, and Ben-Gurion University of the Negev. Through Hillel, students are given opportunities to experience Judaism on their own terms, whether through arts, social action, or Jewish learning. They meet students whose religious backgrounds are different from their own and gain mutual respect and understanding. Experiencing a pluralistic, open community while they are in college may inspire them to help foster a more caring and tolerant society in Israel.

Israeli Hillel chapters are also dynamic international communities. Universities in Israel are a great place for Jewish students who are studying abroad to build a sense of Jewish peoplehood that crosses national boundaries. What has impressed me the most as I have visited Hillel chapters in Israel has been the way students of many cultures mix together. They find a common bond in their all being Jews, and they seem to rejoice in that.

Hillel's transformation, at home and abroad, offers a model for how Jewish renaissance can happen. Similarly, the challenges that Hillel still faces reflect the larger challenges for the North American Jewish community. Even as we celebrate how many more students Hillel has engaged, we have to recognize the truth that most Jewish students still bypass Hillel. This is particularly true of those who are secular and those who are children of intermarried parents. These groups tend to be the most alienated from organized Judaism. Students of patrilineal Jewish descent, for example, know that much of the Jewish world does not consider them Jewish. "All it takes is one insult to push them away," said Rabbi Kerry M. Olitzky, head of the Jewish Outreach Institute, when we spoke about this topic. As at Hillel, all efforts to cultivate Jewish renaissance must be vigilant in ensuring that nobody is told, "You're not really a Jew."

Today, everyone is really a Jew-by-choice. It just doesn't

make sense for us now to differentiate between those born of Jewish parents or of a Jewish mother and other so-called Jews by choice. In a world where so many are choosing not to be Jewish, all who wish to add their voices to our Jewish story must be welcomed and empowered. This is part of the basic policy at Hillel, but at Hillel, as well as across the Jewish world, welcoming must be an active process. We must do more than open the doors to newcomers to Jewish community: We must reach out to them.

I spoke about how this can be done with my son Adam who, as a member of the Hillel International Board of Governors and vice chair of the Board of Directors, works to make Hillel a place that strongly conveys its spirit of inclusiveness. Half the students on campus have one Jewish parent, he said, and many who self-identify as Jews are "walking by the door, not in the door" of Hillel. They think, "I want to bring meaning into my life; I want to make the world a better place," and they want nothing to do with a place that they perceive as preoccupied with whether or not they meet the entry requirements. Hillel should not be talking about who is a Jew or who is marrying or dating whom. The conversation should be about "creating a safe place to explore your morality . . . your ethical structures, and to do that from a vast heritage of intelligent conversation that is based on making the world a better place than you found it. . . . Hillel needs to work with students, no matter who they are or what they are, and make everybody feel comfortable."

Bravo, Adam! Hillel, and all Jewish communities, should

offer young Jews a home, a welcoming space in which together they can learn and dream, debate and celebrate. A
Jewish community should be a space where a shared heritage
does not wall us off from our larger community but provides
us with the grounding, support, and challenge to enable us
to better contribute to it. This community should be a place
where all who choose to enter are welcome: Orthodox and
Reform, children of Jews and of non-Jews, gay and heterosexual, of all races and ethnic backgrounds. Let's encourage
Jewish youth to remake Jewish community as a place where
many voices may support, challenge, and inspire one another.

Birthright Israel: Inspiring Peoplehood

Hillel, an old organization with a new vision, offers young
Jews many ways to get involved in Jewish life and make it
their own. Birthright Israel, which sends young Jews from
around the world on a free ten-day journey to Israel, also has
an ambitious aim: to inspire all young Jews to get excited
about Judaism. It does so briefly, intensively, and with amazing effectiveness. Birthright is the most important new initiative in the Jewish world and deserves wide support.

I first heard about the idea for Birthright over a decade
ago, when I went with Richard Joel to see noted philanthropist Michael Steinhardt. Our quest was to gather major donors
to create a fund that would support projects advancing a Jewish

renaissance. Steinhardt brought up the project idea that most excited him: one that would send college students to Israel for free, a gift from one generation to another. I confess that I didn't see the promise of the idea. It wasn't until perhaps two years later that the project came up again. My brother, Charles, called me from New York while I was summering in Sun Valley, Idaho, to tell me I had to give $5 million—$1 million a year for five years—to the program that hadn't really turned me on. He and Steinhardt were going to go ahead with the idea. Since it was my brother, I said, "OK." Actually, I tried to negotiate, but he was adamant, so I yielded.

Charles and Steinhardt were busy calling and meeting with other philanthropists to do the same thing. Not only that, but they wanted the government of Israel (Ehud Barak was then prime minister) to put up one-third of the cost and the federation system, part of the new United Jewish Communities, to put up one-third as well. Ultimately, Charles and Steinhardt put together a fund of $42 million a year, and the program was ready to go. They called it Birthright Israel, and the restrictions were that participants had to be between the ages of eighteen and twenty-six and that they had never before visited Israel on a peer educational trip.

Since then, more than 100,000 young people have traveled to Israel through Birthright. The program has been an astounding success, by accounts from both participants and researchers.[1] This ten-day journey into history and culture has had a remarkable effect in making secular Jewish young people conscious of their story and eager to learn more.

While there is no magic formula to impart Jewish knowledge and Jewish pride, Birthright, in only ten days, accomplishes a tremendous amount to inspire our youth to look into their Jewish heritage.

What has been puzzling is why the program works so well. I have had students on college campuses all over the United States, Canada, and South America tell me that Birthright "changed their lives." While we live in an era when it's not difficult to be Jewish, it's just as easy or perhaps easier not to be. It's remarkable, then, that these young people come back with a sense of pride and a wish to be more Jewishly involved. So why does a ten-day trip to Israel, with all the security concerns posed by Palestinian terrorism, have such an effect that student after student, sometimes confusing me with my brother, gush gratitude and smile like the cat who just devoured the canary?

I don't have a full explanation. After all, each student is a different person with a different personality. Perhaps meeting with real Israelis and seeing their pride in the accomplishments that have made Israel a successful, formidable country touches something deep inside North American and other Diaspora Jews. I've said all along that Jewish pride is the key not only to Jewish continuity but also to a significant future. To be in Israel, among Israelis who love their country with a contained but deep passion, and then to actually walk where the great heroes of our Jewish history walked, to climb Masada, to see Yad Vashem (the Holocaust memorial museum) and the Western Wall—all this is emotionally powerful. When you add to it, "This is your story, son or daughter," the experience becomes personal, with a special meaning that a non-Jew cannot grasp in the heart.

We Jews have spent thousands of years trying to define just what Jewishness is. It's a religion, say some, but I see this definition as too narrow. It's a nation, it is argued, but the State of Israel is one nation and the rest of us live in others, so that doesn't quite fit. My own feeling is that Judaism is a shared peoplehood and that each of us is our brother's keeper. Jews share a common history that has woven itself through many eras and many cultures, and a common bond that has stayed strong through much hardship. I am reminded of the time when I was in a hotel in Bucharest, on the telephone to the foreign minister of Romania asking him to do what he could for an Iranian Jew who had been incarcerated for being a Jew. The foreign minister wanted to know what the relationship between the two of us was. Although he ultimately intervened on the prisoner's behalf, the foreign minister didn't really understand that while I did not know the person, I felt responsible for him as a fellow Jew. That's Jewish peoplehood, and the Diaspora students who go to Israel sense it even if they can't verbalize it. Suddenly, with a trip to Israel, being Jewish has meaning for them, and they become proud of being who they are.

I met with a number of students from a variety of New York–area schools in order to inquire about their Birthright experiences and to try to understand its power for them. In our discussions, the students described their Jewish connections before, during, and after the trip. Their comments reflect the reality of growing up Jewish for young people today and show the tremendous effect one program can have on students from many different backgrounds. While what they have to say is anecdotal, it conveys their fervent belief in the program, a fervor that never ceases to amaze me as I speak with young people. The Jewish world must understand the importance of Birthright Israel in the renaissance movement. I cannot say enough about how strongly I feel about this.

The students I spoke with all came to Birthright with some Jewish education, which is typical of the North American Jewish college student. For most, also typically, it tapered off in their teenage years. Steve Kleinman, a senior at New York University (NYU), described his upbringing in Florida as "rather secular": He didn't have many Jewish friends, and he dropped out of Hebrew High, a post-bar-mitzvah program. Aviva Garbowit, a recent graduate of the Fashion Institute of Technology, told me that while she had attended Jewish day school in southern Connecticut up to seventh grade, she had had hardly any Jewish education since then and only attended synagogue on Rosh Hashanah and Yom Kippur.

For most of the students I spoke with, their Jewish education had not inspired them to continue to learn. In college, where many find the paths on which they continue through their adult lives, we have a crucial opportunity to reintroduce them to Judaism. Birthright invigorated their interest in Judaism the way nothing had before. "I didn't feel spiritual, and didn't really have any connection with Judaism until last month in Israel," said Aviva. "Something happened," said Michael Wachs, who had just graduated from Hofstra University in Long Island. The students' words remind us that so-called unaffiliated Jews have not rejected Judaism. We simply have not given them meaningful ways to connect.

Why, if their connection to Judaism was tenuous, did these students decide to participate in Birthright Israel? "Free trip," almost all the students responded, some with a touch of embarrassment. There was no wrong reason for choosing to participate in Birthright, I assured them. Michael Steinhardt was right when he insisted that participants should not have to pay, against the objections of those who said that people will not appreciate something they get for nothing. Maybe they will see, as Aviva said she did on her return from Israel, that "the word 'gift' had a meaning." The flame of Jewish identity is something that one generation must pass to the next with love, and without conditions.

While they described their Jewish experience prior to the trip only in relation to religious ritual—that is, having bar and bat mitzvahs and attending synagogue—the students' most meaningful memories of Israel had to do with the land, the people, and the history. Todd Nussen, a Hofstra graduate, had his moment when visiting Yad Vashem in Jerusalem. It connected him to his grandfather, a Holocaust survivor, made Nussen grateful that he was in Israel, and led him to "appreciate Judaism more." In the desert, said NYU senior John Kurta, "I just sat there, and I thought, 'This is why religion started.' There are so many questions you ask yourself when you're out there, just wandering, and you find truths." Steve Kleinman, whose interest in the conflict with the Palestinians had motivated him to attend Birthright, described wandering into the Arab quarter of Jerusalem's Old City and stopping for a falafel. The owner, who was Arab, showed Kleinman pictures of his family and described life in Jerusalem before the intifada. "I remember walking away from there just totally floored by my experience," said Kleinman. "It really hit home, what was going on in the Middle East, what was going on in Israel, why I was there, and all of the humanitarian issues. . . . [The Arabs and Jews] are all one people. We all come from the same place." Being in Israel, where daily life is steeped in Jewish history and culture, transformed the way the students saw their religion and inspired them to explore it further.

The challenge for the Jewish community at large is to build on the enthusiasm about Judaism that Birthright inspires and provide Birthright alumni with meaningful ways to get involved in Jewish life when they return home. Finding ways to link one initiative to another is crucial to making renaissance happen. A single intensive experience can generate excitement and interest, but that will quickly fade if young people cannot find ways to follow up as "real life" resumes.

The partnership between Hillel and Birthright is a terrific example of how synergy between initiatives can work.

Hillel organizes the majority of Birthright trips, and many students from the same universities travel on buses together and share a transformative experience. When they return, Hillel is positioned to build on their excitement with a well-devised program to keep the students connected to Judaism and to each other.

One NYU graduate and Birthright alumna, Lauren Donner Chait, described how the Birthright-Hillel connection can work at its best. Chait attended Birthright her freshman year, on an NYU Hillel trip. She described the bonds the people on her bus formed and, in particular, her friendships with three other young women. Together, the four formed a model of the Jewish community in North America, with one the daughter of a convert, raised Reform; another a nonpracticing Conservative; and another Conservative verging toward Orthodox. Chait herself comes from a family that had belonged to both a Reform and Conservative synagogue. When the friends returned to NYU, they decided to meet every Friday night for Shabbat dinner and for services at NYU's Hillel (to which I am a donor). Chait herself became involved in Hillel in many other ways. As a residential advisor in a dorm, she arranged activities through the Bronfman Center, as the Hillel house is known, for her advisees, Jewish and non-Jewish, including holiday programs and trips to the Jewish Museum in New York City and the U.S. Holocaust Memorial Museum in Washington, D.C. She attended an "alternative spring break" organized by Hillel and the American Jewish World Service, building houses in Yaxuna, Mexico. While it may be unrealistic to expect all students to be as involved in Hillel as Chait, the range of her activities demonstrates the many routes to Jewish involvement that Birthright can inspire. Not only did she attend synagogue, but her Jewish activities also reached outside the Jewish community, into dorm life and social action.

The many Birthright alumni changed the character of the Bronfman Center, Chait said. Before Birthright, "it was [a] more Conservative-type religious atmosphere" that less observant Jews found intimidating. Birthright brought in a whole new population: "Services went from minimal attendance to where you couldn't sit because everyone was coming. I would come because I was going to meet my Birthright friends. And if I'm coming, why not bring six of my other friends? ... It became this whole community for everyone to meet each other and get to know each other." As Chait described, Birthright generates excitement about Judaism, and Hillel offers concrete ways to translate that excitement into action.

Like Hillel, the Birthright program also speaks to a sense of Jewish peoplehood and brings together Jewish youth from around the world. It isn't just American and Canadian students who come to Israel on the largesse of Birthright Israel; students come from all over: from the former Soviet Union, Argentina, Brazil, Uruguay, England, France, and Germany. The excitement the program generates is a great boon to the Diaspora Jewish communities to which they return.

It is also very important for the State of Israel. Long-term support from Diaspora Jewish communities is vital to the security, and even to the prosperity, of Israel, and

Birthright builds that support among the next generation of North American Jews. Today the U.S. government, and especially Congress, is influenced by the Jewish lobby, which has always supported Israel in every conceivable way. Israel is the largest single recipient of U.S. foreign aid, and that is the direct result of congressional action. If today's Jewish youth don't support Israel, the Jewish lobby may lose its influence in the coming years and Israel may lose its vital relationship with the U.S. government. Unlike their parents, who grew up with a sense of pride in the newly formed Jewish state, today's Jewish youth don't automatically feel a commitment to supporting Israel. Anti-Israel activism on campus further challenges this commitment. Birthright gives college students a better understanding of the issues Israel faces and a sense of responsibility for the health and welfare of the Jewish state.

This does not mean that we should cultivate the attitude of "my Israel, right or wrong." I have been both a supporter and a critic of Israel for as long as I can remember. There are two types of criticism: One is loving and constructive; the other is angry and vituperative. During the Carter administration I wrote articles in the press condemning early settlement activity in the West Bank as a hindrance to the peace process, and I have continued to raise my voice against Israeli policies that hinder the creation of an economically viable Palestinian state. Unfortunately, too often those who offer criticism of any kind are called anti-Semites, self-hating Jews, or worse. Young Jews should feel invested in the welfare of the Jewish state and committed to holding it to the standard of justice that they learn is at the heart of Judaism.

Jewish Camping: Cultivating Joy

The next area in which Jews who are dedicated to the renaissance must invest time and money is Jewish summer camps. We know that Birthright works to get college students interested in their Judaism and that Hillel provides them with ways to sustain that interest. But the work that these programs do to create Jewish pride is necessary in part because of a serious lack of quality Jewish education at earlier ages. Jewish summer camps inspire young people to feel proud of being Jewish long before they enter college. At camp, children experience Jewish life as a joy and become more committed Jews, better leaders, and better human beings.

The importance of Jewish summer camps first struck me in a conversation some years ago with Rabbi Avi Weinstein, former director of the Bronfman Youth Fellowships and of the Joseph Meyerhoff Center for Jewish Learning at Hillel. As we discussed how best to reach young Jews today, Weinstein asserted, "What children respond to is a totally Jewish environment."

I suggested, "A Jewish home to begin with?" Weinstein acknowledged the Jewish home is an ideal, but one that is hard to find these days.

Day schools? They are important, he said, but "coercive

environments are not a way to induce a sense of heritage and culture and a love for tradition . . . you don't foster a love of learning by testing someone on it." He added that Jewish educators at day schools often struggle between providing a rigorous Jewish education and teaching a love of Judaism.

As Weinstein told me, "The place that's most sensible to put resources and energy is camps." There kids live Judaism every day. They form close friendships and find Jewish mentors and role models. As they belt out Hebrew songs in the dining hall after dinner or gather for a havdalah ceremony under the stars at the close of the Sabbath, the question "What does Judaism have to do with my life?" becomes irrelevant. Judaism *is* life at camp, and it belongs to the kids.

To get a picture of how the camp experience builds Jewish pride, I spoke with Leonard Robinson, director of the New Jersey Y camps. These camps attract a wide range of Jewish families, from observant to secular. When I asked Robinson about the Jewish content of the programs, he responded, "Here's what I tell the parents. Everything else that we do in camp is unimportant unless the children leave us as better human beings than when they came in." For him, making the children better human beings and building Jewish pride are intertwined. As they form a strong, caring, joyful community, campers grow to understand that the values they put into practice at camp are at the core of Judaism.

Robinson explained the ways that Jewish values are interwoven through the fabric of camp life: "When our kids go to the infirmary to visit someone from their bunk who is sick . . .

they need to know that that's a Jewish value as well as a humanistic value." Kids are taught about Bikkur Cholim societies, Jewish groups that arrange visits to the sick. On Shabbat afternoons, children might engage in a *tzedakah* (social justice) project or an outdoor activity that teaches them about Jewish attitudes toward the natural world.

Campers also experience Judaism in the weekly Shabbat rituals. All Jewish camps make Shabbat a special time, with different meals, decorations, services, and songfests. Campers often look forward to the break from the daily routine and the joyous spirit. At the New Jersey Y camps, Robinson told me, Friday programming stops an hour earlier to set the evening apart and to ensure that the kids know it's different. Campers clean up and put on white shirts. Dinner is "a special Shabbat meal." Services are joyous and participatory, enlivened by singing and guitar music and run by the kids themselves. During the week, the kids are divided into small groups to learn some of the melodies, which include a lot of catchy modern tunes: "We've brought in people from L.A. and all over the country to be our song leaders throughout the summer."

During services, children can also offer a *mishaberech*, a blessing for someone who is ill. Robinson noted that these prayers often include non-Jewish names like McNair and Jones. "Practically everybody has intermarried relatives," Robinson said. That children can find a way to bring their non-Jewish relatives easily into their Jewish world is encouraging. Intermarriage is a reality, and instead of speaking of it as shameful, we should find ways to welcome intermarried families and show them the value of Jewish life.

The Shabbat routine continues through Saturday morning, when campers sleep an extra hour and then eat bagels and cream cheese for breakfast. Services follow. The younger children do not use a Torah but do use the weekly Torah portions, and their service is kept to forty or fifty minutes, "which is about as long as they can sit still." The camps are not *shomer Shabbat* (Sabbath observant)—lights may be turned on and off and people may drive through the camp. No activities that would require children to write are planned, however, and "the few that are a little more observant do not feel that they are left out from the others." Robinson was pleased to report that in their yearly written evaluations campers from unaffiliated, Reform, and Conservative backgrounds all expressed satisfaction with the camps' Jewish content.

For some campers, Robinson commented, camp may be the only time they have observed Shabbat and the only chance we have to reach them Jewishly. At its best, camp can have a tremendous impact in bringing Judaism—whether it be through ritual or through appreciation of ethics—to children who would otherwise have scant Jewish experience. Children sometimes bring home the rituals that they loved at camp, "so parents who have forgotten to train their children are practicing them."

To attract families for whom Judaism is not a top priority, the camps must have quality programs and facilities in all areas, not only those that have to do with Judaism. The New

Jersey Y camps have to compete with well-funded private camps. This is achieved by trying to have "the best waterfront, the best athletics." As the only not-for-profit camps in the area's intercamp sports league, his camps compete against the top: "We try to do the best we can with the resources available; we're just not overly fancy." Children might come for the sports but leave with a stronger Jewish identity as well as a stronger backhand.

Robinson concluded with a note that rang true with me: "My job is to create Jewish grandchildren." His method of reaching this goal is by providing young Jews with an experience that, without preaching, shows them the value in choosing Judaism. Summer camps, where the beauty of Judaism is part of the rhythm of daily life, are an excellent place for this to happen.

As of the summer of 2007, there were some 70,000 Jewish kids attending Jewish nonprofit summer camps. The number of Jewish children of camp age is estimated at 700,000, more than the number of Jews who attend college or university. There has been a marked increase in camp attendance in recent years, but the Jewish community needs to work together to make the numbers even higher and to ensure that all Jewish kids have the opportunity to go to camp.

A leader in making this happen is the Foundation for Jewish Camping (FJC), started by Robert and Elisa Spungen Bildner in 1998. Its mission is "to significantly increase the number of Jewish kids who attend Jewish overnight camps." The Bildners recognized the power of Jewish camping and the need to have a strong national movement to advocate for camps, to build quality camp leadership, to increase enrollment and capacity nationwide, and to develop quality programming. An initiative like this one is Jewish renaissance in action. Two young philanthropists saw a need and dreamed big. Their foundation has generated excitement about camps and has helped bring together diverse Jews across the country who share a belief in the power of Jewish camping. This shared sense of purpose will ultimately spark the flame of Jewish pride for thousands of Jewish children and help them to carry the torch into their own lives.

We spoke with Jerry Silverman, the foundation's director since 2004, about the emergence of Jewish camping as a national movement. Silverman, who was formerly an executive of the Stride Rite Corporation, left the private sector to lead the foundation, and brings his marketing savvy as well as his passion to the field of Jewish camping.

"I think we're on the cusp of something amazing," Silverman said. He described the new energy that was building in the world of Jewish camping. The Jewish community as a whole has begun to recognize the power of camp to sustain Jewish identity, and to seek ways to support it. Camp directors and boards, buoyed by a new appreciation for camps' role in Jewish renaissance, have begun to think beyond the concerns of their individual camps. The first North American Camping Leaders Assembly, convened by the FJC in March 2006, brought together more than 450 Jewish camp professionals and Jewish communal leaders and inspired them to share ideas and resources. In eight communities, lay boards of local camps have come together to strategize for how they might build support for camps, a joint approach that is very different from one in which each camp fends for itself. "People are really wanting to connect; they want to be part of something very large," Silverman said.

The FJC is also a leader in raising the quality and prestige of Jewish camps, for campers and for camp professionals. Silverman described a new program the FJC has initiated, one that brings together camp executives for a rigorous, fifteen-month MBA-style management program. The need for this kind of training is clearly there: "We went through a rigorous admissions process, and we had almost half the field inquire about the program, because nobody's ever invested in the executives," Silverman said. The program's first cohort included camp executives from across the spectrum: "five or six JCC camp directors, four Reform Movement camp directors, an Orthodox camp director, three Conservative, two Young Judaea, and six independent not-for-profit Jewish camp directors." This pluralism in itself is very important in building a shared sense of mission that crosses denominational boundaries. These camp executives may have different methods, but they share the power to give a tremendous gift to Jewish youth: to help them "to celebrate their Judaism in an organic way, in a noncompetitive way, in a way that's just pure joy."

As camps, philanthropists, families, and Jewish communal leaders connect, new initiatives and new ideas flower. Silverman told us about many exciting developments, which demonstrate increased support for Jewish camping, growing cooperation between different groups, and new entrepreneurship and creativity. Philanthropists are helping to make camp more affordable: An anonymous donor has committed $15 million to increase the number of children attending Jewish camps nationally, as part of an incentive program that grants $1,250 to each first-time camper and $750 to those who return for the second year. Different groups have begun to work together: In Colorado, the FJC is facilitating a joint venture project in which a transdenominational JCC camp and a Ramah Camp (which is run by the Conservative Movement) will share a site. The project is sponsored by the Denver community and by the federation. New, specialized camps are taking off: The Ramah Georgia program created a family camp for families with autistic children, which has received such a tremendous response that the camp, unable to offer places to all who are interested, intends to franchise the program to other camps.

There is also a growth of Jewish specialty camps that focus on an art, sport, or other particular skill. Leonard Robinson's New Jersey Y camps, for example, recently developed programs where four out of six periods a day are spent in a particular area, including cinematography, astronomy, baseball, swimming, painting, and jewelry making. The program attracts serious and sometimes notable instructors: Olympic swimmer Lenny Krazelberg, NBA coach Herb Brown, and former Yankee Ron Blomberg have participated in the Y's sports camps. It is this level of quality and prestige that we need to make Jewish camping competitive in every way.

Another model for a Jewish specialty camp can be found in BIMA: the Berkshire Institute for Music and Arts, a camp for high school students that is held on the campus of Brandeis University. The camp was created by Rabbi Daniel Lehmann, founder and head of Gann Academy—the New Jewish High School of Greater Boston, in collaboration with the Bronfman Youth Fellowships staff and alumni. BIMA is an example of how the energy of one initiative can feed into another. Alumni of the Bronfman Youth Fellowships have been teachers and counselors at BIMA and bring their own experience of an intellectually rigorous, pluralistic Jewish community to younger Jews.

At BIMA, students engage in artistic work in their selected major and electives, gather for Jewish learning, ritual, and discussion, and attend cultural events. Participants come from all the denominations, from all over the United States and from Israel. The staff are also diverse: One summer, they consisted of an Orthodox rabbi, an Indian-Jewish painter, and a saxophonist who combines jazz and Jewish music. Jerry Silverman spoke about this model of a truly pluralistic camp focused in a specialty area and held on a college campus as something that could be replicated in many different fields.

Jewish camp is a transformative experience. Those who love it speak of it in an emotional, almost mystical way. "Camping came to me through the glow of my children," Silverman told us. While he did not attend Jewish camp himself, "I just was absolutely transformed by their amazing reaction to their experience at camp, and how it changed them." He quoted his son, who spoke to his synagogue about his summer experience at Camp Ramah. "I love day school," he said. "I really enjoy it and I love to learn." But the Hebrew and Jewish knowledge that he learned at day school was transformed in the crucible of summer camp. At camp, he said, he is able to take "all learning and knowledge that's in my head . . . and put it into practice and live it. And it goes from my head to my heart." Let's make this powerful transformation available to all Jewish children.

The three efforts described in this chapter really work to broaden the reach of renaissance. To increase their impact even further, they need support, including financial support, from across the Jewish community.

Michael Steinhardt, who is at the forefront of efforts to create a Jewish renaissance, keeps asking: Where is everyone else? Why is this very special work being funded by so few? The answer may lie in the fact that too few North American Jews see assimilation as a problem. If one were to propose to the average Jewish community in the United States or Canada that there is a real crisis going on, they would think you were out of your mind. "What crisis?" they would ask. "We've never had it so good." North American Jews are generous. They give to all sorts of institutions—to libraries and hospitals, to universities and prep schools, to symphony orchestras and operas, to ballet and fine arts. They don't give to the renaissance, as yet, because they do not perceive the crisis.

I share with my fellow "mega-donors" a sense of the urgency of our cause and a desire to create and support programs that will effect change on a large scale. The more money you can raise, the broader you can be in your vision, and the more important a project can be in the Jewish universe. We can't do any of this alone.

Donors need to partner up with initiatives that really speak to the needs of young people today. I have been involved with a variety of initiatives, some of which I began myself, others for which my support was sought. In 1996 I started The Curriculum Initiative, which brings Jewish learning and community to students at private schools around the country. These privileged young Jews are our future leaders, and they are largely disconnected from Jewish life. Michael Steinhardt started PEJE, which stands for Partnership for Excellence in Jewish Education. I am a partner, and we are helping communities build more day schools for Jewish children from all denominations. Lynn Schusterman also put together a group, of which I am a member, to take over and put new life into BBYO, the B'nai Brith Youth Organization, a program aimed at teenagers and formerly supported by B'nai Brith. Her late husband, Charles, loved BBYO, and she saw the opportunity to honor his memory and to make a difference. A large fallout in Jewish life is after bar or bat mitzvah, when teenagers who hated Sunday school and whatever other Jewish education they received opt out of Judaism.

My most recent project has been the Web site MyJewish Learning.com. I had the idea for the site while I was enjoying a hot tub at my home in Free Union, Virginia, with my close friend Dr. Neal Kassell. A secular Jew who knows very little about Judaism, he asked me, "If I wanted to find information about Judaism on the Internet, where would I look?" I said, "I don't know. Let me find out." When I looked around on the Web, I found that while there were many Jewish spaces, the informational Web sites that dominated were Orthodox, and that there was nothing on the Internet that would offer a seeker basic information about the range of options and viewpoints that are available in Jewish life.

It seemed vital to me to create something to fill this gap. Today, we turn to the Internet for answers, for information, and for communities of like-minded people. There had to be a place where you could explore an interest in Judaism on your own terms, a place that did not try to "convert" you to a particular kind of Judaism. I wanted to create a site where the only agenda was to foster engagement with Judaism and with Jewish life.

I presented my ideas to my fellow philanthropists and received help in bringing the site to fruition from Lynn Schusterman, Leonard Abramson, and Michael Steinhardt. The Web site offers various levels of information, from the most basic questions to advanced study and inquiry. One can find materials and articles that represent a wide range of perspectives on many topics, from how to celebrate Succot or bake a challah to the origins of the Talmud and the novels of Philip Roth. I am very proud of this site and have been known to say that of all the things that I have done for the Jewish people—securing restitution for Holocaust survivors, emancipating Soviet Jews so that they are able to live dignified lives as Jews—creating this site is one of the most important, because it is about the future of Judaism and talks to young people in their language, that of the Internet.

Chapter 7

JEWISH LEADERS: PASSING THE TORCH TO A NEW GENERATION

L eaders are people who take responsibility on their shoulders. Among North American Jewish youth are many extraordinary young people who are poised to assume positions of leadership in whatever field they choose. While the initiatives I have described foster renaissance by making Jewish life available to large numbers of young Jews, others identify and nurture small numbers of talented individuals in the hopes that they will take responsibility for our Jewish future.

This was my thinking in starting the Bronfman Youth Fellowships in Israel (BYFI), a program that sends twenty-six outstanding Jewish teenagers from a wide variety of backgrounds to Israel for five weeks of learning, travel, encounters with Israeli youth, and meetings with prominent leaders and scholars. I began the program in 1987, when I had grown increasingly frustrated with the fractured and self-serving quality of Jewish leadership in North America. I wanted to create a program that would help to foster a new generation of leaders, one that could see beyond the narrow perspective of particular interest groups to an understanding of the Jewish people as a whole.

The program has been an astonishing success, even if I sound immodest. During the fellowship summers, the twenty-six fellows form a close, respectful community. While some attend yeshivas and others are secular Jews, they study together and recognize that each has something important to add to a discussion of Jewish sources. They work out their own rules for how to observe Shabbat, and while they do not always agree, they learn to respect the choices of their peers. After they have completed the fellowship summer, they stay in touch with each other—over the Internet and through regular alumni gatherings, seminars, and conferences. With the help of the professional staff and The Samuel Bronfman Foundation, the fellows have established their own Board of Directors and award grants to alumni for projects that advance the fellowship's mission.

Over five hundred have now gone through the fellowship, and the oldest are in their late thirties. They are doing amazing things with their lives, making their mark on the Jewish community and beyond. They are journalists, authors, teachers, scientists, professors, lawyers, and businesspeople, and they cite their BYFI experience as tremendously influential, both in inspiring serious change in their own lives as Jews and in motivating them to change the world. These are people who have received many honors and have many educational experiences, yet there is something about this one that touches their lives in a more profound way.

What is the secret to our success? I believe it is due, in part, to the respect for talented young people that permeates all aspects of BYFI. From the start, first-rate young rabbis and educators have run the program. The faculty, in turn, select the best and brightest among Jewish high school students in the United States and Canada and treat their ideas and opinions with respect. As BYFI founding director Rabbi Avi Weinstein once commented, one of the aspects of the program that is revolutionary for the participants is having adults who take them seriously. I have always felt this attitude to be essential in any interaction with youth. If young people are treated with respect, then they will learn to respect themselves.

BYFI never attempts to dictate what the fellows should do with their experience. Some go on to become rabbis, Jewish scholars, and Jewish communal leaders, but directing the fellows into Jewish professions is not the expectation or even the hope of the program. The faculty select the kind of people that will be leaders in whatever they do. If these talented young people are excited about their Judaism and about Israel (with all its faults), they will find ways to bring this excitement into their lives and the lives of others. If, at the age of seventeen, they experience the beauty of a pluralistic community, as they grow up they will seek out these commu-

nities and cultivate their growth. We should not try to mold
the next generation of Jewish leaders in a particular image
but inspire them to envision the future in their own ways.

With BYFI, this inspiration comes from their five-week
encounter with Jewish learning, with the land and people of
Israel, and with each other. Each fellow gives something very
different to the program and takes something different from
it. I am always struck by this when I hear alumni describe
what the fellowship has meant for them. It is fascinating to
see the many ways these young people respond to their experience and the many places they take it.

One of our alumni is the acclaimed young author Jonathan
Safran Foer, whose first novel, *Everything Is Illuminated*, won the
2002 National Jewish Book Award, among other prizes, and
has been hailed as a new masterpiece in Jewish writing. Foer
opened his comments to a meeting of Jewish philanthropists
as follows:

> *I can say with some certainty that I wouldn't be here in this room
> today if I hadn't spent the summer as a Bronfman Youth Fellow,
> and I can say with more certainty that I wouldn't have become a
> writer if I hadn't had that summer experience. I remember one
> afternoon in particular toward the very end of the summer. Every-
> body was exhausted, the weather was particularly hot, and we were
> made to sit in a very small room with a poet I had never heard of,
> named Yehuda Amichai. I entered the room as one person, and I
> left the room as a different person, and I'm much more happy with
> the person who left the room.*[1]

Foer went on to describe himself as an "accidental Jew," who didn't regard his Jewish identity as terribly important until he began to write and found himself writing what, he admits, is a deeply Jewish book. His Judaism, he said, is something that continues to surprise him by its appearance in his life. BYFI did not make him what he is but offered an encounter with Jewish life and literature that would prove to be crucial in his development as a person and as a writer.

Matti Friedman is an alumnus from the same year as Jonathan Safran Foer who came to the program with a different Jewish background and took from it something very different. Friedman, who is now a journalist and a citizen of Israel, writes in a collection of essays about the fellowship that his BYFI summer "has shaped everything that has happened to me since":

> I wasn't fundamentally altered by anything specific that I learned, though fragments have embedded themselves in my memory, like Sharon [Cohen Anisfeld] teaching a Haim Guri poem suggesting that Abraham's near-sacrifice of Isaac has left every one of us with a knife in our heart. I remember that my diet was a balanced one, consisting exclusively of the two major food groups: bread and chocolate spread.
>
> What altered my life was something about the totality of the experience. In Toronto I had been an observant student at a public school, my Jewish and secular spheres packed neatly into separate compartments. Here was an opportunity to get up in the morning (if I went to sleep at all) and be Jewish, along with other people who were Jewish in very different ways, all day. I was not prepared

*to give this up after that summer. It was not that I wanted to study
texts all the time, or talk about what it meant to be a Jew. I just
wanted to be one, and the place to do it, I had seen, was Israel.*[2]

BYFI does not try to convince the fellows to move to Israel, but some have discovered, through the program, that it
is the place for them. If more Israelis felt, like Friedman, the
sense that being Jewish and being Israeli are deeply intertwined, it would be a great boon to the Jewish state.

Jeremy Hockenstein, a 1988 fellow, splits his time between
working as a consultant to Jewish organizations and running
his own nonprofit, Digital Divide Data, that creates sustain-
able jobs for disadvantaged people in Cambodia and Laos. The
two parts of his work may touch different worlds, but both are
informed by his experience with BYFI. He writes: "I sometimes wonder what my life would have been like if I hadn't
been selected as a Bronfman Youth Fellow in the spring of
1988." The fellowship, he said, "instilled in me the importance
of seeking out work which makes a difference. It is particularly
meaningful to me, as my mother was born in a concentration
camp during the Holocaust, that now I am able to help another
people rebuild from their genocide."

Rabbi Angela Warnick Buchdahl writes that her summer,
in 1989, sparked "a love affair with Torah that I still have to
this day":

*As I hit adolescence, questions of my "Jewishness" came to the fore
of my teenage angst over my own identity. It was at this crucial*

point in my life that I was selected to be a Bronfman Fellow. Before that summer, I only knew my small, insular Reform Jewish community in Tacoma, Washington. On BYFI, I roomed with an Orthodox Jew, and an Orthodox rabbi became my inspiration to enter the rabbinate. My trip helped me to understand that my Jewishness was as much a part of me as my being Korean, or being female—as indestructible as my DNA. The summer also issued a greater challenge of how I wanted to be Jewish—what it meant to struggle with God and with life-long learning. Never before my Bronfman summer had I experienced such intellectual and emotional challenges. Never before had I felt so rewarded and grateful to be a Jew.

BYFI did not tell any of these young people how to be a Jew, and the ways they understand and live their Judaism are very different from one another, from Foer's "accidental" Judaism to Friedman's connection to Israel, from Hockenstein's social activism to Buchdahl's "love affair with Torah." What it did was give these interesting, ambitious young Jews an intensive experience of the depth and variety in their Jewish tradition, and the friendships and contacts that would stay with them throughout their lives. We must be confident that our tradition is compelling enough to attract our young leaders to seriously engage with it, and give them opportunities to do so.

To help the next generation of Jews to understand Judaism as a meaningful choice, today's Jewish leaders need to be knowledgeable themselves. Earlier generations of leaders were spurred into action by a sense of connection to the Jewish people, a sense that grew from close-knit immigrant communities and from the experience and recent memory of anti-Semitism. The organizations they created were meant to protect and defend the Jewish people and to enable North American Jews to better their lives. Jewish education was not anywhere near the top of the communal agenda. Today it needs to be our top priority. Young Jews in North America face a difficult question: Why, when we are free to be and do whatever we want, should we choose to make Judaism part of our lives? If Jewish leaders are to meaningfully address this question, they should possess a familiarity with the central texts of Judaism, the source of our ethics. They should be committed to learning throughout their lives and to encouraging others to do the same. They should reach beyond the particular concerns of their denominations or organizations and understand Jewish education as a common goal.

Probably the man who has done the most toward building vision and knowledge in Jewish leadership is Leslie Wexner, founder of The Limited, Inc. (now Limited Brands), who, along with his wife, Abigail, leads the Wexner philanthropies. When asked about his motivation for establishing The Wexner Foundation's leadership initiatives, Wexner said, "Leaders have to recognize that the world changes, and have to realize that the change begins with them. Without talented leaders, there is no future."

To learn about how The Wexner Foundation is effecting

change, I spent some time with Larry Moses, the president of The Wexner Foundation. Les Wexner's leverage point, Moses explained, "has always been leadership, and Jewish leadership is a good two-word definition of our foundation's whole mission." The Wexner Foundation's programs all focus upon "identifying, cultivating, nurturing, and empowering leaders for the next generations in Jewish life." Underlying this mission is "a sense that what was critical in the twentieth century will not be the kind of leadership that will necessarily enable us to succeed in the twenty-first. It's not a matter of replacing leaders; it's a matter of developing new leaders who have a relevant vision reflecting a particular sensitivity to the challenges of their times."

The Wexner Graduate Fellowship Program, aimed at outstanding Jewish professionals, lends prestige to the professional fields of Jewish educational, spiritual, and communal life, and establishes a vital, pluralistic community of leaders. Twenty "outstanding individuals" who are pursuing careers as rabbis, cantors, Jewish educators, Jewish communal professionals, and Jewish studies professors are chosen for this fellowship, which funds their graduate education and provides intensive leadership training institutes and activities for them during their fellowship years. The program is multidenominational, with fellows attending the Orthodox Yeshiva University, the Conservative Jewish Theological Seminary, and the Reform Hebrew Union College–Jewish Institute of Religion, among other institutions. According to Moses, "This program was conceived as an effort to bring the best and the brightest from all denominations and professional interests into a community and create cadres of leadership.... The Jewish community is fairly competitive and noncollaborative, and we're trying to create new generations of professional leaders who have the interests of the larger Jewish community and the Jewish people at heart, even as they pursue the interests of their particular agencies or movements."

Intensive experiences like BYFI and the Wexner Graduate Fellowship are crucial to creating a new cadre of high caliber leaders. Through these programs, young Jews create strong relationships that evolve into informal networks of ambitious, outstanding leaders. "If I had to pick one single piece of my rabbinic education [as most important], it was being a part of Wexner," said Buchdahl, a Wexner fellow. She described how the Wexner conferences allowed her to connect with people who "continue to be professional allies and people that I turn to for advice and gain all sorts of happiness and wisdom from." Religious pluralism is crucial to the dynamism of this network: "The first time we all met, I had that sense of euphoria and giddiness of being with people who were so exciting and so interested in the same issues that I was interested in, and yet very, very different and diverse. We got in huge fights and we argued and we challenged each other, and I felt like there was a great honesty there."

The Wexner Heritage Program, another large-scale endeavor, works with volunteer or lay leaders. Jewish literacy is the focus of this two-year learning program. Participants, most of whom are between the ages of thirty and forty-five, attend eighteen seminars per year over two years in the local community and three out-of-town summer institutes. With the guidance of Jewish luminaries, they study basic Judaism, Jewish history and thought, and contemporary issues in Judaism. Moses described the rationale behind the program: "The idea here is that Jewish volunteer leaders must be armed with a significant level of Jewish learning, Jewish knowledge, and understanding of Jewish history. . . . We can't afford to have Jewish leaders who are Jewishly illiterate."

I boisterously applaud Leslie Wexner's concept. To put it bluntly, North American Jewish leaders in the twentieth century have been for the most part ignorant of Jewish lore, starting with the Bible and including the great thinkers of Jewish history. Synagogue presidents must be more than fund-raisers: They must be models of knowledgeable, proud Jews. Philanthropists must be educated themselves if they are to understand the importance of supporting Jewish education.

The Wexner Heritage Program has done a great deal to help show Jewish lay leaders what Jewish life at its best can look like and inspire them to make a difference. Robert and Elisa Spungen Bildner cite their Wexner experience as part of what inspired them to start the Foundation for Jewish Camping. Laura Lauder, who started DeLeT (Day School Leadership through Teaching), also spoke about the Wexner program as an inspiration. She described how the program "elevated Jewish education . . . adding something that's prestigious, that's highly selective, that puts people in with the greatest teachers, the greatest thinkers and philosophers and minds in American Jewish education today—how much better could it be?" Jewish education is sorely lacking in prestige, and the Wexner Heritage Program shows lay leaders what a difference a quality program can make.

The next generation of philanthropists has begun to step forward to work for Jewish renaissance. Rob and Elisa Spungen Bildner were in their early forties when they started the Foundation for Jewish Camping. The Hillel Board of Governors includes many parent-child partnerships. I am delighted that my sons Matthew and Adam, both in their forties, have begun to take up the reins, Matthew at the World Jewish Congress and Adam at The Samuel Bronfman Foundation and at Hillel, where he oversees the international expansion of the organization. There is a sense of excitement and possibility in Jewish philanthropy as donors across the generations realize that old models of giving may not answer the needs of a new era. Recent initiatives offer innovative ways to inspire younger funders and bring them together for conversation and collaboration. A nonprofit consulting division of the Andrea and Charles Bronfman Philanthropies, 21/64, fosters multigenerational collaboration. It also publishes *Slingshot,* a resource list of fifty of the most creative and effective organizations and leaders across the country to be used by funders who want to support innovative Jewish life. The organization Natan, started in 2002 by four young hedge-fund managers, brings together young donors who pool their funds and bear the risks involved with supporting ideas often overlooked by other Jewish funders. The new young philanthropists are bold, independent thinkers who are determined to bring their own children a renewed Jewish life.

Chapter 8

JEWISH COMMUNAL LIFE: UPDATING OUR INSTITUTIONS

There has been a lot of angst in the organized Jewish community over our high numbers of "unaffiliated" Jewish youth. It is a well-documented fact that many young Jews today do not affiliate with the institutions that were once synonymous with Jewish life—they do not join a synagogue or Jewish Community Center, nor do they give to their local Jewish federation. Many Jewish leaders have bemoaned this phenomenon as a sign of decline in North American Jewish life and sought ways to entice the masses of unaffiliated Jews into traditional institutions.

The problem with the whole idea of "affiliated" and "unaffiliated" is that it depends on an outdated model for Jewish community. The fact that young Jews are not affiliating in the old-fashioned way indicates there is something wrong with our institutions, not that there is something wrong with our youth. We have to let go of old ways of defining what it means to be an involved Jew and look to the kind of involvement that young Jews themselves seek. It takes some imagination to understand that the decline of Jewish institutions does not necessarily mean the decline of Judaism. Our question should not be "How can we get unaffiliated Jews to affiliate?" but "How can we inspire young Jews to understand Judaism as important for their own lives and for the world?" We should not be concerned with keeping Jewish institutions alive but with keeping Judaism alive.

Simply because young Jews are not involved in the same way that their elders were does not mean that they are completely disengaged from Jewish life. While they may stay away from synagogues or Jewish Community Centers, they are clearly interested in Judaism. A recent study of Jews in their twenties and thirties by historian Dr. Ari Y. Kelman and sociologist Dr. Steven M. Cohen observes that while many young Jews may not be affiliated with traditional Jewish institutions, they are celebrating holidays with friends and family, attending Jewish film festivals and concerts of Jewish music, and participating in social action events under Jewish auspices. They want to be Jewish, but on their own terms, as well they should.

The study, commissioned by the UJA–Federation of New York, was based in part on interviews with people at thirteen Jewish cultural events in New York City. These events were all highly successful, with large numbers of young Jews, as well as non-Jews, attending. They included a party on New York's Lower East Side called Slivovitz and Soul, with Yiddish rapping and hora dancing, and Golem Gets Married at the Knitting Factory club, an event that took up the Catskills tradition of a mock Jewish wedding with a cross-dressing bride and groom.

What is it about these events, and others like them, that so appeals to "unaffiliated" Jews? Part of the key to their success seems precisely to be their distance and difference from traditional Jewish institutions. In the study, the authors identify key qualities that the events shared. They were inclusive, and non-Jews were welcome. They were held in nonthreatening public spaces such as theaters, bars, and public parks, not at traditional institutions. They were cultural, rather than religious, in nature. They did not seek participants through guilt, and they mixed traditional ritual with music or performance. The study also describes a sense of irony that pervades these events, as if participants want to distance themselves from Jewish practice even as they engage in it.[1] If those young Jews need distance from anything, it is probably from the Sunday school and Hebrew lessons of their pre–bar and bat mitzvah years and perhaps from the pressure they feel from Jewish institutions about intermarriage and Jewish continuity. I am delighted that young Jews are finding their own ways to connect to Jewish life. We can't force them to come to Jewish institutions, so Jewish institutions have to learn to go to them. When we figure out how to do that, what will our goals be? The answer is not "get them into a synagogue" or to a Jewish Community Center. The answers are dependent on their own desires and hopes. We need to help spark their interest in

Judaism and provide avenues to help them explore it, without conditions. We won't measure our success by checking membership dues but by looking at the vibrancy and variety of Jewish life.

Some young leaders who are frustrated by the limitations of the organized Jewish community have started their own communities that are pluralistic, spiritually dynamic, and attentive to learning and social justice. These rapidly proliferating communities, conceived primarily by young people for young people, are another sign of the growing vitality in Jewish life in North America. They differ in form and focus, but they share an energetic, creative, and welcoming spirit, something that is sadly lacking in too much of Jewish life.

One notable community is Kehilat Hadar (meaning community of splendor or glory), which meets on Manhattan's Upper West Side and gathers for weekly Shabbat services, community service events, learning, and holiday celebrations. We spoke about Hadar with Rabbi Elie Kaunfer, who cofounded the group along with two friends, and Debbie Kaufman, a former organizer and founding member. Hadar started as an attempt by a small group "to create a service, really a Shabbat morning service, that was spirited and egalitarian, with traditional liturgy," Kaunfer said. "At the end of April of 2001, we sent an e-mail to a number of our friends and associates, and that first Shabbat we had sixty people show up at an apartment. We were flabbergasted by the turnout, but very excited. That's when we realized that this actually had some larger impact than simply a few people getting together to daven [pray]."

Hadar clearly spoke to a genuine need for a new kind of Jewish community, even in the Jewish hub of New York City's Upper West Side, and the group grew with amazing rapidity. "We presented something ready-made to a group that was ready to receive, and when they saw that it was something that they were interested in, then they started to say, 'How can I get involved?'" Kaunfer explained.

"It's a brilliant marketing plan," Kaufman added. "Create an excellent program, and people will come. And people will tell other people about it. It's completely e-mail-based. We don't have a letterhead. We don't have posters or a design department. Everything is over e-mail and word of mouth. And it just spread from day one like wildfire."

In Los Angeles, Rabbi Sharon Brous started another community, called IKAR, which means "root" or "essence." IKAR defines itself as a "Jewish spiritual community that stands at the intersection of spirituality and social justice" and has quickly gathered a large following, with hundreds attending Shabbat services each week, the majority of whom are in their twenties and thirties and who were previously unaffiliated with a synagogue.

Brous spoke to us about the two trends that inspired her to create IKAR. The first, which struck her in many conversations with young Jews, was the "deep sense of alienation from the established Jewish community" among Jews in their twenties and thirties, at the same time as they felt a longing for "something rooted and authentic." Most young Jews, Brous said, perceive that the organized Jewish community has a three-part agenda: support Israel because Israel is in crisis, never forget that everyone hates the Jews, and don't marry a non-Jew. She believes that cultivating a sense of connection to and responsibility for Israel is of critical importance, she acknowledges the reality of anti-Semitism, and she does not perform intermarriages herself. But she also believes strongly that a sense of Jewish insularity and self-protectiveness has only served to alienate a generation of Jews. She felt the need for a Jewish community rooted in tradition and in joy, where Jews could engage deeply and authentically with their religion.

The second trend that inspired the creation of IKAR was the rise of terror, AIDS, and global poverty. Particularly after September 11, Brous said that she felt a "profound sense of urgency and discontent" with the state of the world, and a conviction that Judaism has something tremendously valuable to offer. In founding IKAR, she wanted to create a community where prayer and study are fully engaged with the world, where, in the words of IKAR's vision statement, "we search vigorously within our tradition to uncover voices calling for the recognition of human dignity, the loving pursuit of justice, and shalom." To accomplish this is also to speak to the needs of today's Jewish youth. So many young Jews who feel concerned about terror and warfare, Brous explained, also feel invested in engaging with Jewish issues but don't see what one has to do with the other. "I want people to understand how reading the newspaper is a profoundly Jewish act," she said.

When she began IKAR, Brous did not specifically seek

out unaffiliated or disengaged Jews. Yet the community's first demographic study revealed that the large majority fit this category. Most who came to IKAR did not know Hebrew yet were not intimidated by the seriousness of the services. Like New York City's B'nai Jeshurun, which Brous cites as her inspiration, services at IKAR are rich in song and dance. Today's young Jews may be disengaged from traditional Jewish institutions, but as IKAR's success shows, there is a strong desire for a Judaism that, in Brous's words, will "stimulate the intellect, elevate the spirit, and engage seriously in the world."

In Boston, Margie Klein started the Moishe House Boston: Kavod Jewish Social Justice House, where, as Klein described, "activists and Jews of every stripe come together for Shabbat dinners, creative Jewish learning, arts, and social action work." Four people live in the house, and many others are involved in its leadership. Moishe/Kavod House is modeled after Chabad's locally based outreach houses, but while Chabad aims to draw Jews to Orthodoxy, Moishe/Kavod House brings together a pluralistic group of "young Jews who believe that Jewish community and tradition can help us transform our lives and the world." For the activists who gather there, the Jewish tradition offers a way to explore what drives them to work for social justice and to tackle the question that is so central to Jewish sources: "What is our responsibility in the world?" "When activists come together and ask why they do this work, their work changes," Klein said.

Part of the reason she created Moishe/Kavod House, Klein said, grew from her sense that young people often feel "institutionally stranded" after college. As students, they experience an "active Hillel program and dynamic Jewish life" on campus, but when they graduate, they encounter a family-centered Jewish life with no real space for them. Moishe/Kavod House fills this gap for Jews in their twenties and thirties, and provides real leadership opportunities in the postcollege world. Klein also wanted to build a bridge between the commitment to social justice she found in the Reform Movement and the experience of ecstatic prayer she found in Orthodoxy and to create a community where religious engagement and progressive politics could meet. She felt a sense of urgency when, after a year of traveling the country as the leader of a youth voting organization, she saw the power of the Christian religious right. Moishe/Kavod House, in Klein's vision, is a Jewish answer to this phenomenon: a training ground where progressive Jews learn to "catalyze social justice from a faith perspective."

Another community, Brooklyn Jews, was started by Rabbi Andrew Bachman, who used to be director of the Bronfman Center at New York University. When he became senior rabbi at Congregation Beth Elohim, the synagogue became the host for many Brooklyn Jews' events. Bachman is an extraordinary man, very well versed in Jewish texts and an extraordinary teacher as well as community builder. He discovered that while many young Jews in his

Brooklyn neighborhood did not belong to a synagogue, they wanted to learn more about Judaism and participate in Jewish culture and community. Brooklyn Jews began with cultural events, community gatherings, and social action in different locations in the neighborhood: "first Fridays" gettogethers in people's homes; a Chanukah concert called "Jewltide" at a local club; a Purim carnival at a former bathhouse; concerts to raise funds for Hurricane Katrina relief. It grew to include a Monday afternoon Hebrew class for children, which the kids actually enjoy, and High Holiday services held in Prospect Park, Brooklyn. My wife and I attended the service on Rosh Hashanah, and I was delighted to see that the average age was probably thirty-five and that there were young children as well as teenagers. That is what most excites me: to see the next generation of Jews joyfully engaged in Jewish life.

Part of a Jewish philanthropist's role should be to help empower the young people who create communities like those described. Many of the leaders and members of these new communities have been through initiatives such as Hillel, the Wexner Fellowships, and BYFI. (Hadar, Kavod House, and similar efforts have also received grants from BYFI's fund for alumni projects.) While these leadership programs cannot, of course, claim credit for the successes of small communities, they clearly have had a great impact in inspiring their creation. "Programs like Hillel and the Bronfman Youth Fellowships play a big role in empowering young people to think about taking control of their Jewish lives," said Elie Kaunfer. These programs help young Jews to build "serious connections" with others who are excited about Judaism and give them the confidence and the experience to innovate and to lead.

Kaunfer described his own experience as president of Harvard Hillel as "crucial" in inspiring him to found Hadar. It taught him about "pluralism and building a real Jewish community—not just a once-a-month thing." Hillel, he said, has been transformative for a new generation of Jews. When, after graduation, they "find themselves without much access to positions that they had a year ago," they possess the confidence and practical tools to create pluralistic, spiritually vibrant communities of their own. For Margie Klein, the people she met through BYFI and Nesiya, whose summer arts program in Israel brings together North American and Israeli high school students, have been crucial in her organizing efforts. The most important gift a Jewish philanthropist can give to young Jews is the means for them to make Jewish life their own.

Young grassroots leaders have, in turn, offered their insights and experience to efforts by philanthropists to transform Jewish life. Kaunfer is on the advisory board of STAR (Synagogues: Transformation And Renewal), an organization started by Charles Schusterman and after his passing carried on by his widow, Lynn, to bring new life to synagogues. STAR recognizes that an unconventional effort like Hadar should not be seen as a threat to established synagogues, but that it has something to offer them. Synagogue 3000, another effort to reenvision synagogue life, has developed a network of leaders of "emergent sacred communities" that includes Andy Bachman, Sharon Brous, Margie Klein, and Elie Kaunfer. Andy Bachman and Sharon Brous have also been closely involved with Reboot, a fascinating effort funded mostly by the Andrea and Charles Bronfman Philanthropies to invite smart, ambitious young Jews to bring their creative energy to Judaism. Rabbis from established synagogues have sought guidance from these leaders on how to infuse new energy into their own congregations. One generation has a lot to give to the next, and vice versa.

Traditional Jewish institutions must seek guidance from creative young leaders, and some have begun to do so. Young Jews are finding ways to be Jewish outside of traditional Jewish institutions, but that does not mean we have to battle for who controls Jewish life. Kaunfer commented that Hadar has had a very positive response from the organized Jewish community. It's not an "us versus them game," he said.

We need to cultivate this spirit of openness and exchange between new efforts and traditional Jewish institutions. Both are important for the renaissance. While there is exuberant energy outside the established Jewish community, there are tremendous financial, structural, and human resources in our large institutions. These resources can and should be used to educate and empower our youth. While change may happen more quickly in new efforts, existing organizations are capable of making a significant difference in Jewish life if they are willing to adapt to the conditions of the twenty-first century. They need to reach out to young people and invite their ideas and their leadership.

At The Samuel Bronfman Foundation, we have supported new, creative experiments in Jewish life like Brooklyn Jews and MyJewishLearning.com, but we also contribute to large, established organizations, including Hillel and the Jewish federation system. I spoke about our choice to support this range of projects with my son Adam, who has recently joined me in leadership of The Samuel Bronfman Foundation. As he is a young leader and a risk taker (he is an avid "extreme skier"), I wanted his perspective on the choice to work within established institutions as well as outside them.

Adam explained his perspective as follows: On the one hand, working to improve the existing network of Jewish organizations that reaches across North America—the federations, Hillels, synagogues, and Jewish Community Centers—allows us to speak to a majority of Jews in this country and to the institutions that still hold a good deal of power and influence within the Jewish community. On the other hand, small, cutting-edge programs infuse new ideas and energy into Jewish life, and they can be creative and flexible in a way that is difficult for entrenched mainstream institutions. For the renaissance to succeed, it needs to bring both established institutions and new ideas into conversation. As Adam put it, "It's very hard when traditional structures, such as Hillel, are confronted with new paradigms, such as a changing Jewish population on campuses, and really don't have the tools with which to meet the challenge of those changing paradigms." To encourage productive dialogue between old and new, we need "contact between the more traditional and less traditional places within the Jewish world."

Changing traditional Jewish organizations is not an easy task, but it is well worth the effort. Look at the denominations: Most young Jews today grew up with an affiliation to a particular movement. But as they become adults themselves, they increasingly define themselves outside traditional denominational categories. The denominations, and the seminaries where they train their rabbis, will have to recognize this and take a more holistic view of their role in Jewish life. Rabbis need to see themselves as teaching Judaism, not as upholding the tenets of a particular movement. It was the rabbis who, after the destruction of the Second Temple in Jerusalem, replaced the priests as the leaders of Jewish life and kept Judaism from perishing. Today's rabbis should understand the importance of this moment in Jewish history and carry the torch of the Jewish renaissance proudly and with conviction.

What's more, the denominations themselves are no longer the most relevant force in shaping our synagogues. Instead of the large denominational divisions, imagine an entrepreneurial approach to synagogue life, one that encourages the growth of vibrant communities like Hadar and IKAR. Small synagogues of differing styles would compete for "customers," appealing to a variety of needs and desires. Communities of like-minded people would arise, some composed of people who love to daven (pray), others of those who love to sing, and still others of those who love intellectual discussions. Wouldn't it be a wonder if synagogues grew because one person told another, "I have found this marvelous shul. The congregation is totally involved with the service, discussing the meaning of the prayers and the Torah portion. I have learned a lot there. Why don't you come with me next Saturday and find out for yourself?" These same phrases might be uttered about communal singing. Young people are increasingly creating these kinds of communities for themselves, but the numbers are still small. A large-scale reworking of synagogue life as we know it would help Jewish renaissance to reach into all corners of North American life.

Like synagogues, the Jewish federation system (usually referred to simply as "Federation") is another area that once defined community for North American Jews. The federation system is the central address of Jewish charities, and each community has a local federation to which community members donate money. The federations, in turn, finance hospitals, old-age homes, Jewish schools, advocacy for Israel, and Jewish Community Centers. Significant funds go directly to Israel, and another portion is earmarked for other overseas aid. In some cases, a local Hillel will get some financing, and recently some farsighted federations have been financing other engines of the Jewish renaissance. At the beginning of my business career, I led fund drives for Federation, even while I had little other connection to Jewish life. Like many of my generation, I felt a responsibility to give to my Jewish community and to Israel, and the default place to give was to Federation.

Today, however, Federation seems distant from the lives of most Jewish young people. The Jewish federation system, now represented by the national umbrella organization called the United Jewish Communities (UJC), has not kept up with the needs of today's Jewish youth. The UJC was formed in 1999 after a merger of the Council of Jewish Federations with the United Jewish Appeal and United Israel Appeal, and at first had great ambitions to form various subgroups to promote the renaissance and other worthy ideas. Unfortunately, this never happened, and the federation system struggles financially and with its role in Jewish life.

Part of the problem the federation system faces is the result of a generational shift in the way Jews give. We are now facing two trends that make giving by Jews both less generous and less Jewish. The first has been the tendency of the younger generation of major Jewish donors to give large sums of money to hospitals, colleges and universities, art museums, operas, and symphony orchestras on a less parochial basis than did the earlier generation. Younger Jews tend to feel less connected to the Jewish community and more thoroughly integrated into the larger society, and their giving reflects this. It can no longer be assumed that Jews will donate to their local Jewish federation.

Second, those who want to give meaningfully to Jewish institutions prefer to do so on their own, taking active roles in the administration of the institutions and watching the results of their munificence carefully. At most federations, community-appointed professionals decide who gets what, and thus federations are not an appealing draw for donors. Federations should not attempt to dissuade donors from giving to individual institutions rather than to the communal pot but instead work closely with the givers to help them direct their contributions to projects they care about. Too often, the federation leaders throw up their hands in helplessness rather than expressing delight that a new generation wants to be generous, but in its own way. This is a tough lesson to learn, but it will have to be absorbed.

There are a number of federations that are notable exceptions to the problems described. Foremost among them are the Jewish federation of Boston, under the guidance of Barry Shrage; New York, under John Ruskay; and Detroit, which has been very well managed by Robert Aronson. These federations successfully raise funds in their communities and support the renaissance by cultivating new ideas and by supporting outreach, Hillels, day schools, Jewish camping, and Birthright Israel. Federations like these should be models for others and for a Jewish community that works together for Jewish youth.

Jewish Community Centers (JCCs) can also be an important part of the renaissance, as they are positioned to connect with Jews who are not otherwise involved in Jewish life. When the JCC movement began in the mid–nineteenth century with the creation of the Young Men's Hebrew Association (YMHA), it served as a central resource for Jewish immigrants and a place for celebrations within the new Jewish communities in North America. Today, people go to JCCs for their gyms, art classes, nursery schools, and day camps.[2] JCCs must now make Jewish education, culture, and identity a central part of their mission.

The best way to describe a successful JCC is to point to the 92nd Street Y, in New York City (whose name retains part of the original YMHA designation). The 92nd Street Y is known among Jews and non-Jews alike for the sophistication of its cultural programming, both general and Jewish. The Y's Jewish offerings have included talks given by Elie Wiesel, Alan Dershowitz, and Shimon Peres, classes on Jewish spirituality, and a dialogue on what it means to be a Jewish woman today. Rabbi Phil Miller, former director of the 92nd Street Y's Bronfman Center for Jewish Life, told me that people take note of these programs when they come to buy tickets for the general lectures, readings, and events. "Places like the Y are not threatening to people," he said. Many Jews also come for the nursery school, day camp, or fitness center, and the Y attempts to engage them in the rhythms of Jewish life. Miller said he worked closely with the after-school program "to create accessible Jewish possibilities" for children and families. He also collaborated with the Tisch Center for the Performing Arts, for example, pairing Chanukah and Purim festivals with performances of Handel's oratorios on the Book of Esther and the story of Chanukah. "Our job is to take the best of the international events and put them in a Jewish context," Miller said.

Aside from synagogues, denominational bodies, JCCs, and Federation, the Jewish community in North America is made up of a myriad of other organizations. These include international Jewish organizations based in the United States such as B'nai Brith International; the Anti-Defamation League (originally a subsidiary of B'nai Brith); the World Jewish Congress; and the American Joint Distribution Committee. To make it even more complicated, there is an organization called the Conference of Presidents of Major Jewish Organizations, which was organized in the days of John Foster Dulles, who, as secretary of state, was upset with the number of presidents of Jewish organizations who wished to see him about Israel. He suggested that they elect one president to represent them all. This organization is ably run but not as important as it once was, since it can no longer represent all the important organizations, of which there are far more than I can list here.

At one time it was deemed a good thing to have many Jewish organizations, as that meant, it was said, that more Jews would be involved in Jewish life. The trouble with that theory is that organizations chew up money and, even when they no longer have much relevance, they never die. The paid professionals see to that. A Jew in the United States or Canada may belong to a synagogue and any number of other Jewish organizations and pay dues to all of them. These dues are what I call the "Jewish tax dollar," and we have to make sure that it is used efficiently and effectively. This means taking a hard look at what various organizations actually do and eliminating areas of overlap. We must also seek ways to devote more money to Jewish education.

As one step, let's redirect funds used for fighting anti-Semitism toward Jewish renaissance programs. I have publicly stated that it is a waste of the Jewish tax dollar to spend so much money on so-called defense organizations. Anti-Semitism in this country is, for all practical purposes, dead. Yes, there are incidents, but we live in a racist world, and there will always be graffiti and random insults from deranged, sick people. They are a small minority. When a Jew was nominated to be Al Gore's running mate, the miracle was that when they lost, Joe Lieberman was not blamed, nor was his Judaism seen as having cost the party votes.

There are three main defense organizations in North America today: the Anti-Defamation League, the American Jewish Committee, and the American Jewish Congress. All draw support from federations and from the Jewish public. The Anti-Defamation League was founded by B'nai Brith in 1913 to fight anti-Semitism in American society, and it has continued as an independent organization now that B'nai Brith no longer can support it. The American Jewish Congress (which is not connected to the World Jewish Congress) was established to fight for civil rights and found itself on the front lines of the civil rights battles of the 1950s, '60s, and '70s. The American Jewish Committee was originally founded by German Jews to fight pogroms in Russia and to help Americanize the Eastern European Jews who arrived en masse at the turn of the century. The American Jewish Committee has been a major player in fighting anti-Semitism and promoting religious freedom, but now, since anti-Semitism has to a large degree disappeared from the American scene, the Committee finds itself with a large budget, raised from the federation system and individual donors, in search of projects.

A possible solution would be to merge the three organizations and to make Jewish education the beneficiary of the savings. It's not that the work these organizations do is inconsequential but that their objectives might be achieved less expensively. All focus on overlapping issues, including advocacy for Israel, fighting anti-Semitism nationally and internationally, and promoting religious freedom and mutual respect among religious groups. We might put them all together, give them a sensible budget, and put the monies saved into Birthright, Hillel, and Jewish camping, where greater gains can be made. This is easier said than done. The American Jewish Committee tried to effect a merger with the American Jewish Congress some six years ago but failed. The United Jewish Communities (UJC) could force the issue by suggesting that the federation system withdraw its support. The UJC might also appoint a commission to analyze the proliferation of Jewish organizations and recommend a merger here and there, in order to consolidate duplicate organizations. B'nai Brith, for example, should really merge its foreign operations into the World Jewish Congress and close down. Every year B'nai Brith gets less income and has to reduce its activities. Unfortunately, there are jobs lost in mergers, and the professionals resist changes effectively.

Organizations not involved in the renaissance should review what they are doing and ask themselves how they can respond to the crisis in American Jewish life. As an example, are the American Jewish Committee's advertisements in *The New York Times* in support of Israel the best use of their resources? Should they instead be supporting Birthright Israel, Jewish camps, or other initiatives involved in the renaissance? This would be more effective in the long run in building support for Israel. As I have said elsewhere, if young Jews are not committed to Judaism, they will not be committed to Israel.

Finally, if we want real institutional change, all areas of the Jewish community should seek to foster young leadership. In every commencement speech we hear youth described as our future. This is most certainly true, and yet Jewish organizations are loath to act on that dictum. The reason is obvious: No one wants to be usurped and declared redundant, so we hang on, in many cases as long as possible, and keep the young aspirants for Jewish communal life at bay. Perhaps this is the reason that today it's so hard to find first-class Jewish professionals to promote the Jewish renaissance at all levels.

Those of us involved in fostering Jewish renaissance

have a responsibility to see to it that young Jews are given responsibility in the work we do. Perhaps we can create slots for young people where they can learn the so-called ropes and begin to make a real contribution. The work these organizations do must be of sufficient importance— and offer sufficient salaries—to attract smart, ambitious young people, and there must be a strong, bright light at the end of the tunnel so that young people can see ahead to a satisfying career.

In my own life I have had great success in getting top-grade young people to run The Samuel Bronfman Foundation and the World Jewish Congress. I was a young person once, too, and wasn't given the responsibility I thought I deserved. I told myself that I would never make the same mistake. Young people possess energy, imagination, and courage. I will always admire Peleg Reshef, who is now Director of Future Generations at the World Jewish Congress, for his actions at the anti-Zionism and anti-Semitism meeting of the UN World Conference against Racism, Racial Discrimination, Xenophobia and Related Intolerance in Durban, South Africa, in 2001. While major Jewish organizations had stayed away from the conference, Reshef, then a student at the University of Haifa, led a small group of Israeli students who stood up alone to face the hostile crowd. More recently, this same young leader took a group of students to Rwanda to bear witness to the effect of genocide. This is the fearless, passionate spirit that the Jewish community needs.

Jewish youth are more than ready to take up the torch of Jewish life. Where young people have begun to lead, Jewish life has seen tremendous new vitality. Let's have confidence in the strength of our tradition and in the promise of our youth.

Chapter 9

THE JEWISH HOME

When the Second Temple was destroyed in 70 C.E., the Jewish people found themselves without their center of holiness. In response, the rabbis, the intellectual vanguard of the time, found a new place for holiness: the individual home. They called the home a *mikdash ma'at,* a microcosm of the larger sanctuary. As the Talmud tells us, "When the Temple stood, the altar offered atonement. Now, one's table offers atonement."[1] The home, it seems, became the new temple, and our table, the holy of holies.

What does this mean for us today? It suggests that we cannot depend on somewhere, someone, or something else to grant us atonement and bless us but must find our own blessings within ourselves and our homes. We must ask the questions that may be simple to conceive but difficult to practice: How mindful are we when we eat? How do we treat our families? Do we invite guests in? Do we welcome them graciously? Do we teach words of Torah at our table? The home should be the place that not only offers us shelter but also acts as the center of holiness, in our own life and in the life of the Jewish people.

There are many wonderful efforts to cultivate Jewish renaissance and to reach as many Jews as possible. But all the work of well-publicized initiatives will mean nothing if Jews do not bring Judaism into the home. It is in the home, above all, that one generation transmits its culture and values to the next. My hope is that young Jews who are touched by Jewish renaissance will eventually bring Jewish pride to their own children and that Jewish families of all stripes will make a commitment to creating Jewish homes.

"Jewish homes" should not simply mean homes where one or both parents are Jewish. We need so much more than that to pass the flame of Jewish identity to our children. A Jewish home should be a place where children understand Jewish culture as an integral part of family culture. Jewish ethics, tradition, and ritual should be a part of family life, so that from an early age children understand Judaism as something that their parents deeply value. It's not that parents need to be experts in Judaism, but they need to convey their own Jewish pride to their children. Children learn what is important by the subjects that the family speaks about, the events they celebrate, the activities they do together. Parents can't just entrust their children's Jewish education to others and expect the children to embrace Judaism.

Consider the following example: A girl goes away to camp and has a wonderful time celebrating havdalah, the ceremony that divides the Sabbath from the workweek, by the lake. Then she comes home, and on Saturday night she says, "Hey, let's do havdalah." Her mother and father look startled and a bit put out. "What?" they say. "Never mind," says the girl, and that's the end of the story. The girl gets the message that Judaism isn't very important and that havdalah is something that only happens at camp. But if the parents had enthusiastically joined in and said, "Yes! Let's get the candle and the spice jar and do this every week," they would send their daughter the message that Judaism is really meaningful for the whole family. Children understand what is important by what their parents do themselves, not by what they make their children do. Why didn't I go to synagogue growing up? Because my father didn't—he went to the office. If children see their parents opting out of Jewish activities, it is no surprise that they do so themselves when their bar or bat mitzvah comes to an end.

This is the problem with the way supplemental education works. Rabbi Andrew Bachman, who used to run a synagogue supplementary school, described a dynamic where parents would drop off their children, then go to a yoga class or another enjoyable activity, "while their kids labor on a Sunday morning." In cases when their kids acted out, Bachman would hear parents tell them, "You're going to do this, you're going to behave, because I went through it and I did it," instead of conveying to their children that Judaism could be positive and joyful. His inner response, he said, was to challenge parents: "Why don't you light candles together as a family on Friday nights? Why don't you go do Jewish things? Why don't you work on Hebrew together? Why don't you model that you're proud of being a Jew with your child?" If these things are done in the home, "chances are, you're not going to get the kid rebelling about his Jewishness."

Bachman told me that the most successful model for sup-plementary schools is one that engages the entire family, "where you're essentially training the family to do Jewish things together, because ninety percent of the time, it's the family that's together Jewishly." His own young children, at the time of our interview, had never attended religious school, but Bachman said he teaches them Hebrew on Sun-day mornings, they speak Hebrew on Friday nights, and the children "see that we have a great joy to our Jewish existence." Bachman argues that when Judaism is as important a part of "the fabric of the family as a sense of humor or good cooking or going camping or whatever it is that you might do, when being Jewish is as joyous as any of those things, then you're going to succeed at engendering a positive identity."

Bachman also made an important point about intermar-riage and the Jewish home. "I don't want to minimize [inter-marriage] as a challenge facing the Jewish people," he said, "but I can tell you anecdotally from my own synagogue expe-rience, when we would meet, we'd have these Friday night potluck dinners for the different religious school classes, and if it was a mixed-married family, almost universally it was the gentile wife who made sure that the kid showed up at that dinner. The Jewish father wanted actually to have very little to do with it. . . . In many cases, she hadn't even converted. But she tended to come from a tradition where at least she didn't want to run away from who she was, whereas often-times the dynamic with our fellow compatriots is, we run away from ourselves."

To be sure, it is simpler to create a Jewish home if both partners are committed Jews. But a Jewish home can be built by an intermarried couple, and many have done so. What interests me is that if they elect to do so, they are likely to put a great deal of thought into their choices and into their own and their children's Jewish education. As Bachman made clear, the Jewish partner frequently needs to learn about Judaism as much as the non-Jewish partner. Education is what it's all about, for intermarried and inmarried couples alike. If a Jew marries a non-Jew and they decide to bring the children up as Jews, they are likely to learn something about Judaism together. These families need support and encouragement from the Jewish community. As Rabbi Janet Marder expressed in the sermon quoted earlier, we must honor the non-Jewish parent who brings the children to synagogue or Hebrew school and learns to light Shabbat candles and set a seder table.

What does it entail to have a Jewish home? How complicated is it? If you are looking for a place to start, start with Shabbat. The Bible tells us that on the seventh day God rested from his six days of labor to contemplate creation and commanded his people to do the same. Shabbat is a day we all sorely need, a time that is set aside for rest, reflection, and giving thanks. It is a time to teach children, to look at your-self and try to be better. Rabbi Abraham Joshua Heschel wrote of Shabbat: "It is a day on which we are called upon to share in what is eternal in time, to turn from the results of creation to the mystery of creation, from the world of cre-ation to the creation of the world."[2]

The idea of Shabbat observance may be intimidating to some. They know that for religiously observant Jews, the Sabbath, which spans from sundown on Friday to the ap-pearance of the third star on Saturday, is governed by many laws and prohibitions. These laws have been interpreted for modern times from those laid out in the Talmud. You may not work or ask anyone else to work on the Sabbath; you cannot carry any money, or even a pencil or pen, lest you be tempted to buy something or sell something. You are not al-lowed to turn on a switch or drive, since, it is maintained, this is the same as lighting a fire, which the Torah prohibits on the Sabbath.

Sadly, there seems to be a wide gulf in the Jewish world between those who observe the Sabbath and those who don't. More Jews should be able to find a middle ground be-tween strictly observing the Talmudic laws and ignoring the Sabbath altogether. For me, Shabbat is very different than the regular weekdays. On Friday nights, my wife and I light candles and say the blessings for the end of the workweek and beginning of the day of rest. Throughout the Sabbath, I do not exercise, I read, and I mentally engage with Jewish religious subjects. Do I use electricity? Yes, because I do not see turning a switch as violating the spirit of Shabbat. I am not asking anyone to work, nor do I see myself as violating the Biblical commandment against building a fire. Our rabbis have made it too difficult in the modern age to be authentically *shomer Shabbat*. Certainly there are many Jews throughout the world who would agree with my position.

There are a few simple steps to beginning Shabbat observance that could do a lot to strengthen future generations of Jews. First, light the Shabbat candles Friday nights and say the blessings over the wine, the bread, and the coming of Shabbat. Then add two traditions that I learned from my sons Adam and Matthew: a family discussion of the weekly *parsha*, or Torah portion, and a blessing of the children, whether using the traditional benediction or words of your own. The first is a terrific way to bring regular Torah study into the home and to engage in discussions of the ethical questions that arise from the weekly portion. The second sends a tremendous message of love and respect to children, a message that is inextricably bound up in Judaism. There can be something so beautiful about the family greeting the Sabbath together, the children being blessed and feeling loved and safe, the weekly portion being explained and discussed. These rituals acknowledge the family, the Jewish home, and the *something* out there that is greater than we can possibly know.

Is a Jewish home a kosher home? The Torah tells us what to eat in terms of animals, including fish. Reasons for these laws are debated. Some claim they were created for health reasons. More convincing to me is the argument that they were intended to separate Jews from idolaters. The Biblical eating restrictions were a good way to set the Israelites apart from their pagan neighbors. In the Talmud, the laws of kashrut become even more restrictive, making it virtually impossible to eat with non-Jews. Today, it is too much to ask the large majority of Jews to follow the laws of kashrut to the letter. Most young Jews will not elect to live a ghettoized life. They consider their Jewishness to be one facet of their persona but not the only one. They want to meet and eat with others, to stretch their knowledge and their contacts to be as inclusive as possible. This is certainly the way we were meant to behave. We cannot be a light unto the nations if we don't interact with them.

For myself, I obey the Biblical laws of kashrut in that I do not eat pork or shellfish. I view this as a matter of Jewish pride. When my wife and I go out to dinner with people whom we don't know very well, my wife informs them what we don't eat because of our religion. The Jewish dietary restrictions allow me to assert my religious identity, and I think this earns the respect of others.

The Jewish community as a whole needs to encourage Jewish families to bring Judaism into the home. The Lubavitcher Jews are passionately engaged in this project, but their version of the Jewish home is limited to Orthodox observance. There should be more resources available like those on MyJewishLearning.com, which introduces a variety of ways to celebrate Shabbat and the Jewish holidays and offers interpretations of the weekly Torah portion by rabbis and scholars from across the denominational spectrum.

There are also dedicated young Jews, such as Hillel students and members of the B'nai Brith Youth Organization, who would be delighted to go to a home and help families learn rituals and traditions. The Jewish community has many institutions, and these institutions might make it their business to inspire the creation of Jewish homes. Hillel has an active engagement program in the former Soviet Union, where volunteers teach the parents of Jewish students how to prepare and conduct a seder. In many instances, grandparents, with tears of joy, would say how they hadn't heard those songs for many years. Our situation is different in North America— it is not suppression of our religion, but its acceptance, that has caused Jewish practice to fade. But we, too, need active engagement to bring it new life.

Why does the Jewish home matter? It is tremendously important for Jewish continuity, but that answer in itself has not been a motivating force for the majority of North American Jews. Today's young families need to understand Judaism as something that will bring value to their own lives and to the world. What can families gain from the Jewish home? I offer two words: joy and responsibility.

As I was growing up, my own experience of Judaism was joyless. When we observed Shabbat on Friday night, if my father was there (which was not very often), there was no joie de vivre, no celebration of the end of the week and the opening of the day of rest. Saturday meant the dull junior congregation, and Sunday meant Sunday school. Judaism was something I had to do but rarely enjoyed. It was something that set me apart from my peers and that I associated with suffering and prejudice. It seemed that our religion was a collective burden that Jews were obliged to carry, and I did my best to shake it off whenever I could.

When I had children myself, I was still in the midst of a terrible rebellion against my father, and bringing Judaism into the home was the last thing I would do. My children suffered for it. My son Adam speaks about a spiritual vacuum in his childhood, which was especially difficult during the turbulent era of the late 1960s. Without a strong framework in the home "to say there's something better," the world looked to him like a bleak place. I have seven children, and considering their upbringing, I could not have expected that as adults they would become committed Jews. In spite of this, two sons and a daughter, Matthew, Adam, and Holly, are involved with their Judaism. Without Jewish family traditions to draw from, they have created their own, and I admire them tremendously for this.

My own embrace of Judaism happened separately from my children's, as I learned more about Judaism and brought Jewish traditions into my own home. The joy that I have found in this embrace has infused all aspects of my life. It has been a bond between father and children, between grandfather and grandchildren. It has been a source of quiet pride and a sense of larger purpose. It is a joy that I find in all aspects of my Jewish practice, a joy that is fundamental to a religion that celebrates life.

I find joy in the study of Torah and the way it brings people together. My children sometimes join me for weekly Thursday afternoon Jewish text study at my office, and there is tremendous energy in our discussion and debate. There is great joy in teaching Torah to my grandchildren and in trying to respond to their questions. We are commanded to ask questions in Judaism and to teach our children to do the same. Thus, at the seder service on Passover, it is the youngest at the table who is told to ask the question "Why is this night different from all other nights?" In studying our Torah, we find so many guides as to how to live a good life, full of good deeds. As three generations engage with the central texts of our tradition, we enter into a conversation that is deeply rooted in our rich heritage and wide open to the world of today.

There is great joy in the cycle of the Jewish holidays and the sense of renewal that they bring to the year. The High Holidays, which span from Rosh Hashanah to Yom Kippur, offer a tremendous opportunity for introspection and transformation. One High Holiday service period, for example, I decided that my temper was out of control and prayed for the strength to change. I am grateful that my tradition offers us these ten Days of Awe to take stock of what we have done right or wrong, to forgive and be forgiven as the year starts anew. Passover, my favorite holiday, also celebrates rebirth and renewal. The retelling of the Passover story at the seder enacts our people's passage from slavery to liberation, and the festival is ultimately one of celebration, as we rejoice in the great gift of freedom. It is a holiday with universal resonance, when we pray that all people might someday be free.

Holiday celebrations in the home are intricately bound up in the culture of a family and often form our most important Jewish memories. The seders at my parents' home were really the only joyful part of Judaism that I remember from my childhood. I often recall one day when I walked into the kitchen after school. There was my mother, looking helpless. My grandmother had died, and she had always made the *haroset,* as well as the most delicious strudel. It was Mother's duty to make the *haroset,* but she literally hated being in the kitchen and really didn't even know how to boil water. I came to the rescue and volunteered. My mother fled, and it was up to me. I grated some Macintosh apples, chopped some walnuts, and mixed both of them with honey and some decent port wine I had found in the butler's pantry. At the seder, my father commented on the good taste of the *haroset* and asked my mother who had made it. My mother avowed that Edgar had, and I have been making the *haroset* ever since, some sixty years. I have too few happy Jewish memories like this one and gave too few to my own children. I hope that my efforts today will help to inspire others to bring joyful Jewish memories to their own children.

The Talmud teaches that "[d]ivine inspiration eludes an unhappy heart."[3] It is so important that Judaism be joyful. As

Rabbi Arthur Green put it, quality is more important than quantity in acts of faith. If you do not find joy in your practice of Judaism, you should find ways to change it. There are so many different paths in Jewish life. No one should settle for a Jewish practice that feels meaningless and dull.

For years, I struggled with my own sense of disengagement at services. I found the prayers overly repetitive and often thought of Maimonides' criticism of those whose prayer is "extravagant": "[T]hey eloquently continue to praise Him in that manner and believe that they can thereby influence Him and produce an effect on Him."⁴ There is a story of a young man, well versed in the knowledge of the Talmud, who is lolling in bed on a Saturday morning. He tells his father, a successful businessman, that God must be sick of the constant adulation thrown his way. "Would you like it," asked the son of his father, "if every day in every way your employees told you that you were a great businessman, a noble businessman, a caring businessman, a father to his employees everlastingly gracious and mindful of their needs?"

"Of course not," was the immediate reply.

"Don't you think that God must feel the same way?"

The father ripped the covers off the bed and said, "You're going to shul in any event."

Everything changed for me during the High Holidays of 2006, the first time since my bar mitzvah sixty-four years before that I enjoyed and was moved by a service. The previous November I had sat down with Dana Raucher, the executive director of The Samuel Bronfman Foundation, and with Rabbi Darren Levine, executive director of the Jewish Community Project, a dynamic new community in lower Manhattan. I poured my heart out, describing the services I had attended and how boring and repetitive they seemed to me. I went on to describe in broad terms that which I wanted: a service full of music and discussion, where one could learn about the history and structure of the service and where study of text was as central as prayer.

What a joy it was to find that Levine, too, had wanted to create such a service, and he did, beautifully. In a public room in my apartment building, some eighty-five people gathered, including family, friends, and many alumni of the Bronfman Youth Fellowships in Israel. Levine, who is over six feet tall, sat on a high stool. With him was a *chazzan* (cantor), Daniel Leanse, who chanted the prayers and played the guitar, with the backing of a classical cellist and a piano player. The sound was superb. Levine explained the cycle of the Jewish year, showing the congregation that the Days of Awe really start at the beginning of Elul, the month leading up to Rosh Hashanah. Each prayer's significance was explained. There was a prayer for Israel but no sermon.

Kol Nidre and Yom Kippur services followed the same beautiful path. On Yom Kippur morning we had a learning session as we had on Rosh Hashanah, with plenty of participation by the congregants. We broke up at close to 1:00 P.M., then reconvened at 3:00 P.M. for a lively study session on Maimonides' listing of sins. At last, my High Holiday prayers were rich in spirituality and learning, in both emotional connection and intellectual engagement. If creative, spiritual, intellectually engaged services like this one were more broadly available, it would no longer be such a struggle for young people to understand the joy in Judaism, a joy that classic sources tell us is fundamental to our religion. "The authentic spirit of Torah is experienced only through gladness," says one midrash.[5]

To embrace the joy in Judaism is also to take on a deep sense of responsibility, for our fellow human beings and for all creation. Finding joy in our tradition means so much more than simply feeling good. As we observe Shabbat and the Jewish holidays, as we study our central texts, as we gather for prayer and song, we are continually reminded of our responsibility to pursue not just happiness but justice. *Tzedakah,* which comes from a root that means "justice," is the Hebrew word for charity. We are meant to help others not because we are especially loving or good but because it is simply the right thing to do. Maimonides admonished that the greatest charity is to make a person self-sufficient and that the recipient not know who was the benefactor. We should not seek praise or adulation for acts of *tzedakah* but regard them as fundamental to our lives as Jews and as human beings.

Judaism teaches that responsibility is inseparable from freedom. This lesson is present in the Exodus story we tell every year on Passover. As slaves in Egypt, we had no freedom and no responsibilities—we simply did as we were told. In the Sinai desert, before receiving the Torah, we had joyous freedom but no responsibilities. We were an unruly mob of ex-slaves, unable to govern our own desires. When Moses brought down the Ten Commandments from Mount Sinai, he brought a way to distinguish right from wrong. Instead of only obeying orders, we now had to take responsibility for our actions. In the Ten Commandments, we found a higher justice than the will of a pharaoh or king, and the means to seek this justice was now in our hands.

There's a wonderful midrash in which Moses goes up to heaven and faces the angels, who are terribly upset. They want to know why God has given the gift of Torah to Moses rather than to them. Moses is at first afraid to answer, lest the angels kill him, but he puts his hand on God's celestial throne for protection and explains: Angels don't need to be told right from wrong, but human beings do.[6] God's gift gave us the much-needed means to live together in peace and justice. This lesson is so important to understanding the value of our central texts. Whether one believes that God created the Torah or that we created God to add force to our ethical precepts, Judaism offers a human-centered approach to ethics, in which we are called to take responsibility for our actions, for each other, and for our world.

The rituals of the Jewish life cycle bring this sense of responsibility home. When young men and women are called to the Torah on the occasion of the bar or bat mitzvah, they are told that they are now responsible for knowing the difference between right and wrong. As they are welcomed into the rich world of Jewish text and tradition, they are welcomed as individuals who think, learn, and question for themselves. It is so important that children understand their bar or bat mitzvah not as the moment when they are released from the captivity of Hebrew school but as the joyous celebration of the Torah and the responsibility that arrives with it.

As we get older and start families, we take on more responsibility. At every stage, in every year, in every week, our Jewish tradition offers the means to grow and learn, to take stock of how we are doing and explore how we can do better. It reminds us, also, that we must take responsibility not only for ourselves and our families but also for a world that is badly in need of healing. It can be overwhelming to confront the conflict and suffering around the globe and to figure out how to address it in our homes and in our lives. The Jewish home can help families to rejoice in something better than what we see around us and to take responsibility for making a difference. As we celebrate life with food, wine, and song, we never forget that we are God's partners in creation, responsible for keeping the planet in good condition. As we celebrate the bonds of family and of peoplehood, we also remember the Torah's teaching that we must love the stranger, "because you were strangers in the land of Egypt." The stranger, remarkably, is the only person the Torah commands us to love. We are commanded to honor our parents but not to love them. Perhaps this is because family love comes easily, but we need to be reminded of our bond with those who are different.

This imperative is particularly strong for Jews in the

United States and Canada. With our struggle for our own rights won, we enjoy unprecedented freedom and security. With this freedom come great responsibility and great opportunity. We must direct our resources not just toward the needs of our own people but also toward helping others. As we seek to foster a renaissance in Jewish life, we must seek to foster a community whose learning, prayer, and traditions inspire us to ethical action. As we address the reality of a declining Jewish population in North America, we must also address the persistent question of why Judaism matters. A Judaism whose only purpose is to preserve itself is a Judaism without purpose.

I once asked the late Arthur Hertzberg (a scholar, rabbi, and dear friend) whether it was really important that Judaism stay alive. His response was that Jews have done so much and that we have so much more to do. Our world is badly in need of healing. Humankind is doing great damage to the future of our planet with fossil fuels that create acid rain, smog, and global warming. We have a Jewish responsibility to lead in the effort to undo the damage. We must also guard against the horrors of genocide, which we witness even after the lesson of the Holocaust. We must make good on our vow of "Never again" and raise our voices to urge the governments of the world to stop what took place in Rwanda, Bosnia, and Cambodia and that which is now taking place in Darfur and Chad.

We must also be leaders in bringing an end to the violence between the Israelis and the Palestinians. There has been a war going on in the Middle East for as long as Israel has been a state, and its neighbors have tried to destroy it. Israel has defended itself with a force that reflects its fear of destruction and its determination to survive. That does not excuse actions that deny Palestinians their basic human rights. The concept "my Israel, right or wrong" is flawed. Let our voices be heard in insisting that an economically viable Palestinian state must be the result of Israeli initiatives. Jewish ethics is the great contribution of Judaism to the world, and the treatment of the Palestinians fails to be ethical or just. Both Israelis and Palestinians have suffered heartbreaking losses, and hope for peace must be kept alive.

Speaking of the wrongs that persist in a free society, Abraham Joshua Heschel often said: "Some are guilty. All are responsible." We cannot condemn others without taking responsibility ourselves. We have the knowledge of right and wrong, and the freedom to act. We have the resources, both spiritual and material, to make a tremendous difference in the world. Let us pass the torch of Jewish life to our children, so that they may face the darkness in our world with hope, not fear, and carry the light of our tradition with pride and with purpose.

Earlier in the book I quoted Dru Greenwood, who in describing her choice to convert to Judaism told me, "I felt like I was coming home." As we bring Judaism into the home, we also make it possible for Judaism and Jewish community to become a home to many.

What does a home at its best offer? In a fast-moving, diverse society, home is where we find mooring. It is at home that we consider our central values and teach them to our children, where we develop the ethical base that will guide our actions in the wider world. Judaism and Jewish community can and should be such a home. The rhythms of Shabbat and the Jewish holidays make space in our lives for reflection and celebration, for remembering our past and for looking ahead. Jewish community offers a place where people of all ages and backgrounds gather to mark the cycle of the year and of our lives. Our tradition of text study opens the way for ethical inquiry.

Jewish community has always provided a sheltering home for Jews in times of danger and need. But the quality that we most need to foster now in our Jewish home is not just security but welcome. Those who seek a home in Judaism should find a community and a tradition that ushers in its guests with warmth and pride and that celebrates diversity of background and opinion. Those who marry Jews should find in Jewish community a loving family that welcomes them without conditions.

For all who care about the Jewish future, the task of reaching out must start from within. The Jewish community is no longer sustained by the ancient temple altar and won't be sustained simply by writing a check to a Jewish cause or by dropping your child off at Hebrew school. Our Jewish institutions must work to foster Jewish renaissance, but true change will only occur when all Jews realize that Judaism matters and take steps to bring their tradition into their lives, into their homes, and into their hearts.

I was once asked, while visiting a Hillel in Miami, to describe the most spiritually significant moment in my life. My answer was twofold. The first was during my bar mitzvah, when the rabbi, whom I loved, put up his hand and gave me the priestly blessing. The next was at the age of twenty-one or twenty-two, when I saw my grandfather for what I knew would be the last time and asked if he would do the same. In his room, he put on his tallis, lit a candle, and blessed me. At the time, I was angry and disengaged from Judaism. Yet I found the blessing deeply moving. In it, I felt a deep connection to my grandfather, to my forebears in ancient times, and to a cycle of existence far greater than I could imagine. It was the blessing of Judaism, so old and yet so alive.

My only regret in life is not having given a Jewish home to my children. I have been making up for it ever since. I pray that my grandchildren, and generations to come, will know a Jewish life that is rich in learning and in spirit, a Jewish life that is a blessing to the world.

JEWISH RENAISSANCE INITIATIVES

There is a place for everyone who wishes to become involved in Jewish life. The following listings provide additional information about many of the initiatives that are mentioned in this book. They represent only a sampling of the projects and programs that are helping to make Jewish renaissance a reality and doing important work in areas that include education, social justice, spirituality, leadership, and outreach. For a more extensive listing of organizations and for ideas about how to be a part of a Jewish renaissance, MyJewishLearning.com offers additional resources.

ALMA HEBREW COLLEGE

www.alma.org.il

A liberal arts center in Tel Aviv for the study of Hebrew culture and contemporary Jewish identity. Its New York affiliate, Alma New York (www.almany.org), creates community through the integration of arts, classic text study, and modern scholarship. Its programs cross not only denominational lines but also religious and secular lines.

AMERICAN JEWISH WORLD SERVICE (AJWS)

www.ajws.org

Dedicated to alleviating poverty, hunger, and disease among the people of the developing world regardless of race, religion, or nationality. The AJWS has been a leader in responding to the crisis in Darfur, Sudan, where the ongoing genocide urgently requires action.

BERKSHIRE INSTITUTE FOR MUSIC AND ARTS (BIMA)

www.brandeis.edu/bima

Brings talented teens together for four weeks in the summer to cultivate a vibrant, pluralistic environment brimming with artistic discovery and Jewish experiences. A BIMA summer experience allows teens to hone their artistic skills, live and discover in a diverse Jewish community, and explore who they are as artists.

BIRTHRIGHT ISRAEL

www.birthrightisrael.com

Provides the gift of first-time peer-group educational trips to Israel for Jewish young adults ages eighteen to twenty-six. Its founders created this program to send thousands of young Jewish adults from all over the world to Israel as a gift in order to diminish the growing division between Israel and Jewish communities around the world, to strengthen the sense of solidarity among world Jewry, and to strengthen participants' personal Jewish identity and connection to the Jewish people.

THE B'NAI BRITH YOUTH ORGANIZATION (BBYO)

www.bbyo.org

A youth-led, worldwide organization that provides identity-building and leadership development programs for Jewish teens.

Programs in sixty communities around North America provide innovative opportunities for teens to connect with one another, take part in community service projects, navigate the college admissions process, and travel the world.

THE BRONFMAN YOUTH FELLOWSHIPS IN ISRAEL (BYFI)

www.bronfman.org

Offers a five-week summer program in Israel that educates and inspires exceptional young Jews from diverse backgrounds to become active participants in Jewish culture throughout their lives and to contribute their talents and vision to the Jewish community and to the world at large.

BROOKLYN JEWS

www.brooklynjews.org

An open resource for those seeking a meaningful connection to Jewish life, culture, and practice, centered at Congregation Beth Elohim in Brooklyn, New York. Participants take the lead in social programming, Shabbat celebration, social action projects, and Jewish learning.

COMBINED JEWISH PHILANTHROPIES (CJP)

www.cjp.org

The Boston Jewish federation, Combined Jewish Philanthropies, has placed a strong emphasis on outreach, working hard to make local Jewish communities more welcoming both to intermarried families and to disengaged Jews. Some have credited these efforts for the recent finding that the Jewish population in the Boston area has increased, with a significant majority of children of intermarried couples being raised as Jews.

CONGREGATION BETH SIMCHAT TORAH
www.cbst.org
New York City's synagogue for the New York metropolitan area's 200,000 gay, lesbian, bisexual, and transgender Jews, as well as families and friends.

THE CURRICULUM INITIATIVE (TCI)
www.tcionline.org
The leading Jewish educational organization serving independent high schools. Through extracurricular programming, school presentations, and professional development, TCI strengthens Jewish students' Jewish identity and nurtures school communities' appreciation for the Jewish heritage.

DRISHA INSTITUTE FOR JEWISH EDUCATION
www.drisha.org
A New York City–based institute that creates opportunities for women in Jewish scholarship, education, and leadership. Drisha offers a wide variety of educational initiatives, including full-time programs with a leadership development track, summer institutes, a summer high school program, a bat mitzvah program, continuing education programs, and community lectures.

FOUNDATION FOR JEWISH CAMPING (FJC)
www.jewishcamping.org
The central address for information about, and advocacy for, nonprofit Jewish overnight camps, providing leadership, expertise, and financial resources to camps, campers, and their families across North America.

HEBREW COLLEGE RABBINICAL SCHOOL

www.hebrewcollege.edu/html/rabbi.htm

A transdenominational rabbinical school, located in the Boston area, that offers a rigorous five-year full-time course of study leading to rabbinic ordination within a model *klal Yisrael* community.

HILLEL: THE FOUNDATION FOR JEWISH CAMPUS LIFE

www.hillel.org

Provides opportunities for Jewish students at more than 500 colleges and universities to explore and celebrate their Jewish identity through its global network of regional centers, campus foundations, and Hillel student organizations. Its mission is to enrich the lives of Jewish undergraduate and graduate students so that they may enrich the Jewish people and the world.

IKAR

www.ikar-la.org

A Jewish spiritual community in Los Angeles that stands at the intersection of spirituality and social justice.

INTERFAITHFAMILY.COM

The online resource for interfaith families exploring Jewish life and the grassroots advocate for a welcoming Jewish community. This resource is for everyone touched by interfaith relationships where one partner is Jewish, on every topic of interest to them, and for everyone who works with and cares about them.

JEWISH BOOK COUNCIL

www.jewishbookcouncil.org

The central address for all information about Jewish literature.

This organization publishes a quarterly magazine including reviews of the latest books of Jewish interest and through its Web site keeps you updated on book programs nationwide.

JEWISH FEDERATION OF METROPOLITAN DETROIT
www.thisisfederation.org

Detroit is a Jewish community where the federation is really working to promote Jewish renaissance. Particularly notable is its work to promote day schools in the community, including the admirable Jean and Samuel Frankel Jewish Academy of Metropolitan Detroit.

JEWISH OUTREACH INSTITUTE (JOI)
www.joi.org

Through national conferences, publications, and informational resources, JOI has helped foster the creation of scores of Jewish outreach programs from coast to coast. Its vision is that the future of the North American Jewish community will be determined by the warmth, wisdom, and caring with which we welcome and engage the intermarried families and unaffiliated Jews into our midst.

KEHILAT HADAR
www.kehilathadar.org

An independent, egalitarian community in New York City that is committed to spirited traditional prayer, study, and social action.

KEHILAT SHIRA CHADASHA
www.shirahd.org.il

A religious community in Jerusalem that embraces a commitment to halacha (Jewish law), *tefillah* (prayer), and feminism.

MECHON HADAR

www.mechonhadar.org

Aims to revitalize communal life—animated by prayer, study, and social action—among young Jews in America. Founded by three of the leaders of Kehilat Hadar, it offers two main initiatives: Yeshivat Hadar, a full-time community open to men and women looking to engage in intensive Torah study, prayer, and social action, and the Minyan Project, which provides education, consulting, and networking for independent prayer communities.

MOISHE HOUSE BOSTON: KAVOD JEWISH SOCIAL JUSTICE HOUSE

www.kavodhouse.com

An innovative project to create community for Jews in their twenties and thirties and connect them with social action and community-building opportunities in Boston and beyond.

MYJEWISHLEARNING.COM

The central Internet Web site for learning about Judaism. MyJewishLearning.com is a transdenominational site of Jewish information and education geared toward learners of all ages and educational backgrounds.

THE NATAN FUND

www.natan.org

A philanthropic network of young Jews seeking both to inspire other young Jews to donate money Jewishly and to fund innovative projects that help effect change in the Jewish community in the United States and Israel.

PARTNERSHIP FOR EXCELLENCE IN JEWISH
EDUCATION (PEJE)
www.peje.org
A collaborative initiative of philanthropic partners whose goal
is to strengthen the Jewish day school movement by increasing enrollment in Jewish day schools in North America.

SHALOM HARTMAN INSTITUTE (SHI)
www.hartmaninstitute.com
A research and leadership training institute in Jerusalem whose
mission is to revitalize Judaism, strengthen Jewish identity, and
foster religious pluralism by providing scholars, rabbis, educators,
and lay leaders of all denominations with tools to address the central challenges facing Judaism today.

STAR (SYNAGOGUES: TRANSFORMATION AND
RENEWAL)
www.starsynagogue.org
Helps synagogues deepen their connection with the American
Jewish community through congregational innovation and leadership development. Its centerpiece is Synaplex, which provides synagogues with grants to host a series of dynamic, multifaceted events
on Friday evenings and Saturdays.

21/64
www.2164.net
A nonprofit consulting division of the Andrea and Charles
Bronfman Philanthropies, which offers services to individuals, families, businesses, foundations, and federations in times of generational
transition.

UJA–FEDERATION OF NEW YORK

www.ujafedny.org

The New York Jewish federation has been a leader both in providing social and humanitarian services and in promoting Jewish education.

WEXNER GRADUATE FELLOWSHIPS

www.wexnerfoundation.org

Funds the graduate education of outstanding future rabbis, cantors, Jewish educators, and Jewish studies professors and provides them with leadership training and networking opportunities.

WEXNER HERITAGE PROGRAM

www.wexnerfoundation.org

Offers Jewish volunteer leaders two years of intensive study in basic Judaism, Jewish history and thought, and contemporary issues in Judaism.

INTERVIEWS CITED

RABBI ANDREW BACHMAN, senior rabbi, Congregation Beth Elohim, Brooklyn, NY; founder, Brooklyn Jews

ADAM BRONFMAN, managing director, The Samuel Bronfman Foundation, New York, NY; member of the Hillel International Board of Governors and vice chair of the Hillel Board of Directors

RABBI SHARON BROUS, founding rabbi and spiritual leader, IKAR, Los Angeles, CA

RABBI ANGELA WARNICK BUCHDAHL, cantor, Central Synagogue, New York, NY

RABBI DAVID ELLENSON, president, Hebrew Union College–Jewish Institute of Religion, and I. H. and Anna Grancell Professor of Jewish Religious Thought, New York, NY

RABBI ARTHUR GREEN, rector, Hebrew College Rabbinical School; Irving Brudnick Professor of Philosophy and Religion, Hebrew College, Newton, MA

DRU GREENWOOD, director of synagogue renewal, UJA–Federation of New York; director (1991–2005), the William and Lottie Daniel Department of Outreach at the Union for Reform Judaism, New York, NY

RABBI DAVID HARTMAN, founder and codirector, Shalom Hartman Institute, Jerusalem

DR. TOVA HARTMAN, professor of education, the Hebrew University of Jerusalem; founder, Kehilat Shira Chadasha, Jerusalem

DR. PAULA HYMAN, Lucy G. Moses Professor of Modern Jewish History, Yale University, New Haven, CT

RICHARD JOEL, president, Yeshiva University, New York, NY; president and international director (1988–2002), Hillel: The Foundation for Jewish Campus Life, Washington, D.C.

DEBBIE KAUFMAN, founding member, Kehilat Hadar, New York, NY

RABBI ELIE KAUNFER, executive director, Mechon Hadar; cofounder, Kehilat Hadar

MARGIE KLEIN, founder and coordinator, Moishe House Boston: Kavod Jewish Social Justice House, Brookline, MA

RABBI SHARON KLEINBAUM, senior rabbi, Congregation Beth Simchat Torah, New York, NY

RABBI DANIEL LEHMANN, founder and headmaster, Gann Academy—The New Jewish High School of Greater Boston; founding director, Berkshire Institute for Music and Arts (BIMA) at Brandeis University, Waltham, MA

RABBI SHIRA MILGROM, senior rabbi, Congregation Kol Ami, White Plains, NY

RABBI PHIL MILLER, director (2001–2004), Bronfman Center for Jewish Life, 92nd Street Y, New York, NY

LARRY MOSES, president, The Wexner Foundation, New Albany, OH

RABBI KERRY M. OLITZKY, executive director, Jewish Outreach Institute, New York, NY

FELIX POSEN, founder and president, the Posen Foundation, London, England

LEONARD ROBINSON, executive director, New Jersey YMHA-YWHA camps, Fairfield, NJ

RABBI HAROLD SCHULWEIS, rabbi, Valley Beth Shalom, Encino, CA

LYNN SCHUSTERMAN, chair, Charles and Lynn Schusterman Family Foundation, Tulsa, OK

DR. GARY A. TOBIN, president, Institute for Jewish & Community Research, San Francisco, CA

RABBI AVI WEINSTEIN, director (1997–2004), Joseph Meyerhoff Center for Jewish Learning, Hillel: The Foundation for Jewish Campus Life; executive director emeritus, Bronfman Youth Fellowships in Israel

RABBI AVI WEISS, founder and president, Yeshivat Chovevei Torah Rabbinical School, New York, NY; senior rabbi, Hebrew Institute of Riverdale; president and founder, AMCHA—The Coalition for Jewish Concerns, Bronx, NY

RABBI ERIC H. YOFFIE, president, Union for Reform Judaism, New York, NY

BIRTHRIGHT ISRAEL ALUMNI: Steve Kleinman, Aviva Garbowit, Michael Wachs, Todd Nussen, John Kurta, Lauren Donner Chait

NOTES

Biblical quotes, unless otherwise noted, are from the Jewish Publication Society's *Hebrew-English Tanakh* (Philadelphia: Jewish Publication Society, 1999), second edition.

INTRODUCTION

1. Pirkei Avot 2:5. Translation by Sharon Cohen Anisfeld.

2. Pirkei Avot 1:1. Translation by Sharon Cohen Anisfeld.

3. Exodus 23:9.

1. A GOLDEN AGE FOR NORTH AMERICAN JEWRY?

1. Arthur Hertzberg, *The Jews in America: Four Centuries of an Uneasy Encounter* (New York: Touchstone, 1989), 153.

2. Commission on Jewish Education in North America, *A Time to Act: The Report of the Commission on Jewish Education in North America* (Lanham, MD: University Press of America, 1991).

2. ABRAHAM AND SARAH'S TENT: RETHINKING INTERMARRIAGE

1. The Biblical and Talmudic texts in the preceding discussion are quoted from Avi Weinstein's curriculum, "Welcoming Guests," available on Hillel's Web site, at www.hillel.org/jewish/textstudies/learn_love/guests .htm. The interpretation is mine.

2. Genesis Rabbah 48:9.

3. Genesis Rabbah 60:16.

4. National Jewish Population Survey, 2000–2001, at www.ujc.org (accessed February 2008).

5. Jeri B. Zeder, "Still Jewish! What It Means Now to Be a Jewish Woman in an Interfaith Marriage," *Lilith* magazine (summer 2005), 13.

6. Pearl Beck, principal investigator, *A Flame Still Burns: The Dimensions and Determinants of Adult Jewish Identity Among Young Adult Children of the Intermarried* (New York: Jewish Outreach Institute, June 2005).

7. Genesis 12:2 and 12:7, as quoted in Donniel Hartman's essay.

8. Deuteronomy 7:4.

9. Donniel Hartman, "Who Is a Jew? Membership and Admission Policies in the Jewish Community," *Judaism and the Challenges of Modern Life*, edited by Moshe Halbertal and Donniel Hartman (London; New York: Continuum Press, 2007).

10. Janet Marder, "Blessing for Non-Jewish Spouses—Yom Kippur Morning" (Congregation Beth Am, Los Altos Hills, CA, September 25, 2004), at www.betham.org/sermons (accessed February 2008).

11. Ruth 1:16.

12. This reading of Ruth and Naomi's story was suggested by Rabbi Dianne Cohler-Esses, who also made suggestions for many of the Biblical and Talmudic quotations in the book.

3. A NEW JUDAISM FOR A NEW GENERATION: ENGAGING THE DISENGAGED

1. Alexander Schindler, "Outreach: The Case for a Missionary Judaism," address to the board of trustees of the Union of American Hebrew Congregations (Houston, TX, December 2, 1978); full text is available at www.urj.org.

2. Harold Schulweis, "The Mirror of Inreach and Outreach," at www.vbs.org/rabbi/hshulw/mirror.htm (accessed February 2008).

3. Harold Schulweis, *For Those Who Can't Believe: Overcoming Obstacles to Faith* (New York: HarperCollins, 1994).

4. Abraham Joshua Heschel, *The Sabbath: Its Meaning for Modern Man* (New York: Farrar, Straus and Giroux, 1975).

5. Peter L. Berger, *The Heretical Imperative: Contemporary Possibilities of Religious Affirmation* (Garden City, NY: Anchor Press/Doubleday, 1979).

6. Arthur Green, *Ehyeh: A Kabbalah for Tomorrow* (Woodstock, VT: Jewish Lights, 2004).

7. Mordecai Kaplan, *Judaism as Civilization* (New York: Macmillan, 1934), 178.

8. See article about Dahaf Institute poll by Sever Plocker, "The New Israeli Jew," *Yediot Ahronot* (April 2, 2007), available on their English-language Web site, www.ynetnews.com.

4. RESPECT, NOT TOLERANCE: EMBRACING JEWISH DIVERSITY AND DIFFERENCE

1. United Synagogue of Conservative Judaism, "Frequently Asked Questions," at www.uscj.org (accessed February 2008).

2. Rachel Adler, *Engendering Judaism: An Inclusive Theology and Ethics* (Philadelphia: Jewish Publication Society of America, 1998), xiv.

3. Deuteronomy 24:1.

4. Rabbis Elliot N. Dorff, Daniel S. Nevins, and Avram I Reisner, "Homosexuality, Human Dignity & Halakhah: A Combined Responsum for the

Committee on Jewish Law and Standards," approved December 6, 2006, at www.rabbinicalassembly.org/law/new_teshuvot.html (accessed February 2008).

5. Leviticus 18:22.

6. Gary A. Tobin, Diane Tobin, and Scott Rubin, *In Every Tongue* (San Francisco: Institute for Jewish & Community Research, 2005).

7. Babylonian Talmud, Eruvin, 13b.

5. "GO AND LEARN": OUR PLAN OF ACTION

1. Babylonian Talmud, Shabbat 31 a.

6. HILLEL, BIRTHRIGHT ISRAEL, AND JEWISH CAMPING: BRINGING JEWISH LIFE TO LARGE NUMBERS OF JEWISH YOUTH

1. For recent research, see Brandeis University's Maurice and Marilyn Cohen Center for Modern Jewish Studies Web site, at www.cmjs.org.

7. JEWISH LEADERS: PASSING THE TORCH TO A NEW GENERATION

1. Audio recording, Opening Plenary, 2006 Jewish Funders Network International Conference, at www.jfunders.org/programs/2006-jfn-international-conference/conference-audio (accessed May 2006).

2. This quote, as well as the following ones, comes from a collection of essays about the Bronfman Youth Fellowships presented to me to celebrate the fellowship's eighteenth year, and my seventy-fifth birthday, in 2005.

8. JEWISH COMMUNAL LIFE: UPDATING OUR INSTITUTIONS

1. Steven M. Cohen and Ari Y. Kelman, *Cultural Events and Jewish Identities: Young Adult Jews in New York* (New York: National Foundation for Jewish Culture, 2006).

2. Jewish Community Center Association, "The History of the JCC Movement," at www.jcca.org/about_us.html.

9. THE JEWISH HOME

1. Babylonian Talmud, Chagigah 27a.

2. Abraham Joshua Heschel, *The Sabbath: Its Meaning for Modern Man* (New York: Farrar, Straus and Giroux, 1975).

3. Jerusalem Talmud, Sukkah 5:1.

4. Moses Maimonides, *Guide for the Perplexed*, translated by M. Friedlander (New York: Dover, 1956).

5. Midrash, Tanna D'Bei Eliyahu Zutta, chapter 17.

6. Babylonian Talmud, Shabbat 88b–89a.

ABOUT EDGAR M. BRONFMAN

Edgar M. Bronfman is a renowned philanthropist, business-man, and Jewish leader. He led the Seagram Company Ltd. for more than thirty years. Through The Samuel Bronfman Foundation, named in memory of his father, he supports many initiatives that inspire a renaissance in Jewish life. He is founding chairman of Hillel: The Foundation for Jewish Campus Life and has played a key role in transforming Hillel into a vibrant international organization. In 1987, he founded the Bronfman Youth Fellowships in Israel, which educates and inspires future leaders from diverse Jewish backgrounds. The Curriculum Initiative, which Bronfman created in 1996, supports Jewish students in independent high schools and introduces school communities to Jewish culture and ethics. In 2001, Bronfman founded MyJewishLearning.com to serve as an online center of learning for Jews of all denominations and levels of knowledge.

Until June 2007, Bronfman also served as president of

the World Jewish Congress (WJC), an international federation of Jewish communities and organizations whose primary goal is to preserve and foster the worldwide unity of
the Jewish people. Working with the WJC, he advocated
for the release of the Prisoners of Zion from the USSR and
convinced Pope John Paul II that the establishment of a
Carmelite convent near Auschwitz would be an affront to
Jews worldwide. In 1998, Bronfman succeeded in winning
restitution for Holocaust victims whose assets had been held
in Swiss banks. He has also served as president of the World
Jewish Restitution Organization, which is devoted to the return of property and wealth owned by Jews who perished in
the Holocaust.

Bronfman has been recognized for his leadership by or-
ganizations, universities, and governments around the world.
In 1999, President Clinton awarded him the Presidential
Medal of Freedom, the United States' highest civilian honor.